Essential Histories

The First World War
The Western Front 1914–1916

Essential Histories

The First World War

The Western Front 1914–1916

Peter Simkins

OSPREY
PUBLISHING

First published in Great Britain in 2002 by Osprey Publishing,
Elms Court, Chapel Way, Botley, Oxford OX2 9LP

Email: info@ospreypublishing.com

Every attempt has been made by the Publisher to secure the
appropriate permissions for material reproduced in this book. If
there has been any oversight we will be happy to rectify the
situation and written submission should be made to the
Publishers.

ISBN 1 84176 347 0

Editor: Rebecca Cullen
Design: Ken Vail Graphic Design, Cambridge, UK
Cartography by The Map Studio
Index by Michael Forder
Picture research by Image Select International
Origination by Grasmere Digital Imaging, Leeds, UK
Printed and bound in China by L. Rex Printing Company Ltd

02 03 04 05 06   10 9 8 7 6 5 4 3 2 1

For a complete list of titles available from Osprey Publishing
please contact:

Osprey Direct UK, PO Box 140,
Wellingborough, Northants, NN8 4ZA, UK
Email: info@ospreydirect.co.uk

Osprey Direct USA,
c/o Motorbooks International, PO Box 1,
Osceola, WI 54020-0001, USA.
Email: info@ospreydirectusa.com

www.ospreypublishing.com

This book is one of four volumes on the First World War in the
Osprey Essential Histories series

Contents

Introduction

More than 80 years on, the First World War, and in particular the struggle on the Western Front, continues to fascinate us and to cast long shadows over the world in which we live. For Britain, the effort and sacrifice required to create and sustain her first ever and biggest ever citizen army, and to help defeat the main enemy in the decisive theatre of operations, left profound emotional and psychological scars which influenced much of the nation's subsequent history and which are still evident today. Countries such as Australia, Canada and New Zealand all came of age during the conflict and now have their own established national interpretations of the significance and conduct of the Great War. In Britain, at least, the inclusion of the subject in the national syllabus, the blossoming of organisations such as the Western Front Association and the frequency of battlefield tours all indicate that interest in the First World War is actually growing. This is hardly surprising, since it has touched and affected the history of countless individuals and families.

Despite all this interest and attention, popular perceptions of the Western Front remain almost totally dominated by images of futile frontal attacks in the Flanders mud and of doomed youth being slaughtered at the whim of uncaring 'butchers and bunglers' who sat in remote châteaux many miles behind the lines. Another persistent view of the First World War, especially among American historians, maintains that the German Army was immeasurably superior to the Allied armies in weapons, tactics, training and command and that its eventual defeat came about through no fault of its own. A third, and equally pervasive, strand of opinion suggests that Germany should have been attacked by means of a less costly, indirect approach, 'through the back door' – in other words, causing Germany's collapse by knocking out her allies, Austria, Bulgaria and Turkey.

In fact, there was no real alternative to the Western Front. While the bulk of the German Army chose to stay in Belgium and northern France it had to be tackled and beaten there. As the last year of the war would show, it was Germany that shored up her allies, not the reverse. There were, of course, incompetent British and Allied generals and the ordeal of the front line soldier on the Western Front was often as terrifying as traditionally portrayed. So how, in the end, was the German Army defeated?

Anglocentric historians have tended to understate the colossal contribution and sacrifice made by the French in the first half of the war. However, in the last decade or so, scholarly research in Britain and the Commonwealth has revealed that there was also a well defined and more or less continuous learning curve in the British and Dominion forces as they expanded and that, in the final analysis, their collective tactical and technological improvement was a key factor in the ultimate Allied victory.

This volume, the first of two dealing with the Western Front, focuses on the years from 1914 to 1916, a period of trial and error in which a trench warfare stalemate descended on the battlefields and both sides strove to find an antidote to the defensive superiority of modern firepower. These years also represent a time of painful adjustment, for all the major belligerents, to the voracious demands of 20th century warfare. The increasingly important role of women in industry and the spreading involvement and intervention by government in all aspects of daily life were common to British, French and German society.

By the close of 1916 the balance of *military* power on the Western Front was shifting. The British and Dominion formations were becoming more effective and experienced while the fighting capacity of the French and German armies, sapped

Men of the 2nd Battalion, Argyll and Sutherland Highlanders, wearing early pad respirators as protection against gas, June 1915. (IWM)

by their efforts over the preceding two years, had started to decline.

Chronology

1914 **28 June** Archduke Franz Ferdinand assassinated in Sarajevo.
5/6 July Germany gives Austria-Hungary 'blank cheque' of support against Serbia.
23 July Austro-Hungarian ultimatum to Serbia.
25 July Serbia mobilises.
26 July Austro-Hungarian mobilisation against Serbia. Russia enters 'period preparatory to war'.
28 July Austria-Hungary declares war on Serbia.
29 July Germany demands immediate cessation of Russian mobilisation preparations.
30 July Russia orders general mobilisation in support of Serbia.
31 July Russian mobilisation begins. Germany proclaims 'threatening danger of war' and issues ultimatum to Russia.
1 August Germany declares war on Russia and orders general mobilisation. France orders general mobilisation.
2 August German ultimatum to Belgium demanding the right of passage through her territory. German troops invade Luxembourg.
3 August Germany declares war on France.
4 August Germany invades Belgium. Britain declares war on Germany.
6 August French troops move into Upper Alsace.
7 August Germans capture Citadel at Liège.
14 August Battle of the Frontiers begins.
23 August Battle of Mons. British Expeditionary Force begins retreat.
26 August Battle of Le Cateau.

5–10 September Battle of the Marne.
13–27 September Battle of the Aisne.
14 September Falkenhayn takes over control of German operations from Moltke.
15 September 'Race to the Sea' begins.
10 October Antwerp falls to the Germans.
18–30 October Battle of the Yser.
19 October–22 November First Battle of Ypres.
29–31 October Turkey enters the war on the side of the Central Powers.
3 November Falkenhayn succeeds Moltke as Chief of the German General Staff.
5 November Britain and France declare war on Turkey.
17 December French winter offensive begins in Artois.
20 December French winter offensive begins in Champagne.

1915 **4 January** French offensive in Artois ends.
10–12 March Battle of Neuve Chapelle.
22 April Germans use poison gas for the first time on Western Front.
22 April–25 May Second Battle of Ypres.
25 April British, ANZAC and French troops land on Gallipoli.
9 May Allied offensive begins in Artois. Battle of Aubers Ridge.
15–27 May Battle of Festubert.
23 May Italy enters the war on the side of Allies.
25–26 May Formation of a coalition Cabinet and creation of Ministry of Munitions announced in Britain.

25 September Allied offensive in Artois and Champagne. First use of poison gas by British at Battle of Loos.
5 October British and French forces land at Salonika.
11 October Bulgaria enters war by invading Serbia.
19 December Haig replaces Sir John French as Commander-in-Chief of the British Expeditionary Force.

1916 **9 January** Evacuation of Gallipoli peninsula completed.
27 January First Military Service Act becomes law in Britain, introducing conscription for single men aged between 18 and 41.
21 February Battle of Verdun begins.
25 February Germans capture Fort Douaumont at Verdun.
24 April Easter Rising in Dublin.
25 May Second Military Service Act becomes law in Britain, extending conscription to married men.
31 May/1 June Naval Battle of Jutland.
1 July Battle of the Somme begins.
27 August Romania enters the war on the side of the Allies.
29 August Hindenburg succeeds Falkenhayn as Chief of the German General Staff with Ludendorff as 'First Quartermaster General'.
15 September British use tanks for the first time at Flers-Courcelette on the Somme.
24 October French counter-attack at Verdun. Fort Douaumont recaptured.
25 November Battle of the Somme ends.
7 December Lloyd George succeeds Asquith as British Prime Minister.
12 December Nivelle replaces Joffre as French Commander-in-Chief.

The road to war

The route which led the major powers of Europe to war in 1914 was long and tortuous, with many complex and interwoven factors eventually combining to drive them into a protracted and cataclysmic struggle. Among these factors were new naval and military technology, colonial rivalries, economic competition and irreconcilable national ambitions. However, perhaps the most important and obvious turning point towards a general European conflict was the Franco-Prussian War of 1870/71. That limited confrontation had seen the humiliating defeat of France and the unification of Germany under Prussian leadership. The sudden emergence of the German Empire, which as part of the spoils of victory took the provinces of Alsace and Lorraine from France, brought about a fundamental shift in the European balance of power. Germany's subsequent and accelerating progress towards economic ascendancy only intensified the anxieties of her neighbours and competitors.

For the best part of two decades, between 1871 and 1890, the new European status quo was not seriously challenged, thanks to the diplomatic dexterity and deviousness of Otto von Bismarck, the German Chancellor, in keeping France isolated. When Bismarck left office in 1890 it was not long before a fresh series of unpredictable currents began to erode the foundations of his carefully constructed Continental system. A rapid deterioration in Russo-German relations and a rapprochement between Tsarist Russia and Republican France compelled Germany to strengthen her existing links with the Austro-Hungarian Dual Monarchy, so ensuring that she possessed an ally to the east. While Germany was undeniably the dominant partner in this particular alliance, she would pay a heavy price for a policy that

tied her more closely to a dilapidated empire that was itself finding it increasingly difficult to curb the nationalist aspirations of its diverse subject peoples in south-eastern Europe. The potentially explosive situation in the Balkans was made more dangerous by the decline of Turkish influence there, offering both Austria and Russia (the self-proclaimed protector of the southern Slavs) tempting territorial and political prizes in the region. In seeking to exploit such opportunities, Austria and Russia each embarked upon a course which could only end in confrontation. The rise of Serbia added yet another hazardous element to an unstable regional mixture. Serbia had been infuriated by Austria's annexation of Bosnia and Herzegovina in 1908 but had herself gained influence and territory as a result of the Balkan Wars of 1912 and 1913, giving Austria, in turn, mounting cause for disquiet and irritation.

With the departure of Bismarck, the belligerent and erratic Wilhelm II – who had become *Kaiser* (Emperor) in 1888 – soon spurred Germany to follow a more aggressive path in international relations. France, already determined to avenge the disaster of 1870/71 and win back her lost provinces, was further alarmed by Germany's developing industrial and military muscle; Russia too had grounds for concern about an Austro-German alliance that not only threw an ominous shadow along her western frontier but was likely to counteract Russian interests in the Balkans.

The first, and probably the most significant, crack in the edifice erected by Bismarckian diplomacy came in 1892 with the removal of its cornerstone – the isolation of France. That year, Russia and France concluded a military agreement – reinforced by additional talks in 1893 and 1894 – under

Kaiser Wilhelm II, Emperor of Germany 1888–1918. (IWM)

which each promised to come to the other's aid if either were attacked by Germany.

This change from Bismarck's *Realpolitik* (politics of realism) to the *Weltpolitik* (world policy or politics) of Kaiser Wilhelm II ultimately forced Britain to review her relations with other leading players on the European and world stage. Admittedly, Germany was not the only power that made Britain uneasy. Recurrent tension in her relations with France and Russia, previously her chief naval competitors, had caused Britain to pass the Naval Defence Act in 1889 in order to safeguard the supremacy on which her national security and prosperity rested. The Act embraced the doctrine that the Royal Navy's establishment should, at any given time, match the combined naval strength of any two other countries. The maintenance of this 'Two Power Standard' became more difficult as the United States and Japan also began to overhaul Britain industrially and to build ocean-going fleets. Britain was, however, content to stick largely to her policy of 'splendid isolation' so long

as the balance of power in Europe was not imperilled and no single nation became too dominant or threatened Britain's security by making a hostile move into the Low Countries towards the Channel ports.

Britain was, in fact, relatively friendly with Germany for much of the last quarter of the 19th century, not least because Queen Victoria's eldest daughter was married to the German Crown Prince, Frederick, who succeeded to the imperial throne in March 1888. Frederick died from cancer after reigning for barely three months, and the accession of his estranged and impulsive son, Wilhelm II, heralded fresh competition with Britain for colonies and overseas markets as the new Kaiser sought world power status for Germany. Even so, it was the German Navy Laws of 1898 and 1900 that did most to alienate Britain. Shaped by the German Naval Secretary, Rear Admiral Alfred von Tirpitz, with the Kaiser's enthusiastic support, these measures disclosed Germany's intention to construct a fleet, including 38 battleships, within 20 years. Regarding Britain as Germany's 'most dangerous naval enemy', Tirpitz envisaged the German fleet as a political pawn which would strengthen his country's hand in world affairs. To this end he wished to provide Germany with sufficient capital ships to mount a genuine challenge in the North Sea and give her the capability of inflicting such damage on the Royal Navy that the latter would fall below the 'Two Power Standard'. The launching of 14 battleships in Germany between 1900 and 1905 inaugurated a naval arms race that would enter an even more menacing phase when Britain launched the revolutionary turbine-driven 'all-big-gun' battleship HMS *Dreadnought* in 1906.

German backing for the Boers during the South African War of 1899–1902 hastened the demise of Britain's earlier isolationist policy. Since the United States Navy was not obviously aimed *directly* at her interests, Britain, in 1901, deliberately abandoned any attempts to compete with growing American naval power. The following year an Anglo-Japanese treaty was signed, considerably reducing British anxieties in the Far East and enabling Britain to concentrate more warships in home waters. In 1904 the *Entente Cordiale* greatly strengthened British diplomatic and, later, military ties with her traditional rival, France. A similar understanding was reached with Russia in 1907, once Japan's victory in the Russo-Japanese War of 1904/5 had all but removed the long-standing Russian threat to India. Thus before the end of the first decade of the 20th century Britain had swung noticeably towards the Franco-Russian alliance.

The understandings with France and Russia did not constitute formal agreements and neither did they commit Britain irrevocably to go to war in support of either power, but she was now at least morally bound to France and Russia in opposition to the Central Powers, Germany and Austria. Any unforeseen incident involving one or more of these countries might well ignite a general conflagration which, because of the rival alliance systems, could engulf them all. In these circumstances it would certainly not have served Britain's interests to stand aside and allow Germany to conquer France and occupy the Channel ports. Therefore, despite all the contradictions in Britain's new international stance, the possibility of her participation in a European war on the side of France and Russia was – as Germany should have been well aware – far from remote.

Diplomatic manoeuvres, opposing alliances and naval rivalry were not the only ingredients which rendered the European powder keg more explosive and conditioned

King Edward VII takes a salute during his State visit to Paris, May 1903. The visit helped cement improving relations between Britain and France. (IWM)

European alliances before and during the First World War

- Central Powers, August 1914
- Allies, August 1914
- Neutral countries subsequently aligned with Central Powers
- Neutral countries subsequently aligned with Allies
- Countries originally aligned with Central Powers, declared neutrality at the outbreak of war, then later joined Allies
- Countries which remained neutral

nations and peoples for armed conflict. The spread of education and adult literacy in the decades before 1914 also saw the rise of a popular press ready to glamorise deeds of military valour or take an unashamedly jingoistic line when reporting foreign affairs. Chauvinism and aggressive imperialism were similarly encouraged by capitalism. Fashionable ideas about 'national efficiency' and concepts such as 'Social Darwinism' emphasised the survival of the fittest and fostered the belief that war was a purifying ordeal necessary to counter any signs of national decadence and moral degeneration. As most political and military leaders erroneously thought that should war

come, it would be short, statesmen were generally more willing to solve international disputes by military rather than diplomatic means.

All the individual national motives for conflict and collective failures to halt the slide into the abyss cannot, however, conceal the primacy of Germany's responsibility for war in 1914. In the often savage debate that has raged since the work of Professor Fritz Fischer in the 1960s, historians have disagreed about the extent to which Germany positively sought and planned the conflict in advance; but few have denied that Germany was its mainspring. For Prussian aristocrats, the officer class and industrialists, war held great attraction as a means of negating or diverting attention from the increasing internal influence of the Social Democratic Party. It would also enable Germany to forestall the modernisation and improvement of the Russian Army, expected to be complete by 1916/17. Since Germany's impressive economic expansion had not yet been rewarded by world power status, a successful war would simultaneously end her diplomatic and military encirclement and bring her the geopolitical influence she felt she deserved.

On 8 December 1912, the Kaiser summoned his senior military advisers to a war council. The fact that some of the conclusions reached on this occasion coincided with the actual events of 1914 has led Fischer and other historians to view the meeting as evidence that Germany's leaders took a conscious decision there and then to go to war within 18 months. The importance of the meeting in this respect may have been exaggerated, but there is no doubt that the Kaiser and the military-political-industrial élite wanted hegemony in Europe and were fully prepared to contemplate war, with all its attendant risks, as the quickest way of realising their ambitions. This in itself represented a serious enough threat to European peace but the situation was made infinitely more hazardous by the iron grip which the Kaiser and his circle maintained on the reins of power in Germany. Whereas considerable checks and balances were imposed upon the political and military leaders of Britain and France by their respective parliamentary systems, the German Army was essentially beyond civilian control. Its senior officers were directly responsible to the Kaiser, and neither the Chancellor nor the state secretaries (or 'ministers') were ultimately answerable to the Reichstag, the German parliament. In other words, those in Germany who were most willing to plunge Europe into war in order to deal with their own internal and external difficulties, and to assure Germany's standing in the world, were subject to the fewest effective restraints.

The opposing armies

Germany's strategic ambitions and the unique status her armed forces enjoyed within society helped to ensure that, until 1916 at least, the Imperial German Army would be the dynamo of the First World War. It was Germany's war plan that did most to determine the course, if not the nature, of the conflict. The plan itself had been shaped originally, between 1897 and 1905, by Count Alfred von Schlieffen, then Chief of the German General Staff. Schlieffen's overriding aim had been to enable Germany to deal successfully with the strategic nightmare of a two-front war against Russia and France, should such a situation arise. However, by appearing to offer a feasible solution to this problem, the plan reduced the Army's fears of a two-front war and, correspondingly, strengthened its willingness to accept the risks of such a conflict. In these respects, one could argue that the Schlieffen Plan, instead of being a mere precautionary measure, actually increased the likelihood of a general European struggle.

Schlieffen estimated that, should Germany have to face both France and Russia, the latter would be slower to mobilise and deploy, giving Germany a vital margin of some six weeks in which to overcome France by means of a massive and rapid campaign in the west. As soon as France was defeated, Germany could then transfer the bulk of her forces to the east to tackle Russia. There was a danger, nonetheless, that the fortresses along France's north-eastern frontier might fatally delay the German Army's lightning western offensive. Accordingly Schlieffen resolved that German forces must cross a narrow strip of Dutch territory known as the 'Maastricht

Appendix', then sweep through neutral Belgium before driving into north-western France. The pivotal role in the campaign was given to five armies deployed between Metz and Holland, totalling 35 corps in all. The most powerful forces were allocated to the extreme right wing of the offensive. One army here was expected to swing round to the west of Paris, on the outer flank of a colossal wheeling movement which was intended to take the opposing French armies in the rear before trapping them up against their own frontier. It was anticipated that, on

Count Alfred von Schlieffen, Chief of the German General Staff 1891–1905. His war plan, with modifications, largely shaped German strategy in 1914. (IWM)

the outbreak of war, the French would advance immediately into Lorraine, so two weaker German armies were assigned to the left, or eastern, wing. Their task was to contain the French movement and even fall back slowly, if required, in the hope of luring the enemy forces beyond any point from which they could seriously interfere with the planned German encirclement.

Colonel-General Helmuth von Moltke, Schlieffen's successor, made several key alterations to his original plan between 1906 and 1914. Though a diligent and painstaking officer, Moltke was also introspective and suffered from bouts of low self-confidence. He was especially anxious about the potential threat to German communications which the expected French thrust into Lorraine would pose. Consequently, most new divisions created after 1906 were assigned to the German left wing rather than the crucial right. Once seven times stronger than the left, the right wing became only three times stronger as a result of Moltke's changes. Of equal significance was his decision to abandon the projected movement through Holland while sticking with the planned advance through Belgium. This decision was doubly unfortunate for it not only complicated the problems of deployment – squeezing the right wing armies into a tighter initial bottleneck – but it also failed to eliminate the considerable diplomatic and strategic disadvantages almost certain to ensue from any German violation of Belgium's neutrality. Historians have rightly observed that, even as originally conceived, the Schlieffen Plan was unworkable, as it paid insufficient heed to the problems of over-extended supply lines, inadequate communications systems, the fatigue of troops and the unpredictability of battle. It also miscalculated the speed of Russian mobilisation and the level of resistance which Belgian forces and civilians would offer. However, it is equally true to say that the changes wrought by Moltke did little or nothing to improve it and further undermined its already tenuous prospects of success.

Conscription, the bedrock of the German military system, permitted her to increase the size of her army swiftly, from a peacetime strength of around 840,000 to more than 4,000,000 trained soldiers when war was declared. Able-bodied young German males first joined the *Landsturm* at the age of 17; at the age of 20 they were called to the colours for full-time military training, which lasted two or three years, depending upon their arm of service. Thereafter they would pass into the reserve for four or five years and then carry out additional spells of service with the *Landwehr* and *Landsturm* until they reached 45. The *Landwehr* and *Landsturm*, upon mobilisation, would undertake defensive duties on lines of communication, and the reservists were alternatively recalled to regular units or formed new reserve corps and divisions that could confidently be used as front line formations. The system, especially the employment of reservists, was to give the Germans a significant advantage over the French Army in some critical sectors along the front in the opening weeks of the war.

In the summer of 1914 German infantry training was in the midst of a transition from close-order to open-order tactics – a factor that would cost their infantry dear. However, the army as a whole was excellently trained, had a solid nucleus of highly capable non-commissioned officers and could claim a clear superiority in its light, medium and heavy howitzers – weapons which would quickly prove their worth in the operations to come.

The French military system was likewise based upon conscription. In 1913 compulsory service had been extended to three years with the colours, then 14 in the reserve. Because her population was smaller, France had to call up a bigger proportion of the nation's men, including colonial recruits, to attain even a semblance of parity with Germany. At the outbreak of war, France was able to muster approximately 3,680,000 trained soldiers but had fewer reserve formations than the Germans mobilised.

In the wake of the humiliation of the Franco-Prussian War French military doctrine

German infantry photographed on manoeuvres before the First World War. (IWM)

had been recast. The most important figure in this process was Lieutenant-Colonel (later Marshal) Ferdinand Foch. His teachings as Chief Instructor (1896–1901) and Commandant (1908–1911) of the *Ecole Supérieure de Guerre* placed the 'will to conquer' firmly at the core of the French Army's creed and inspired an almost mystical faith in the primacy of the *offensive à l'outrance* (attack to the limit). The same gospel was preached by one of Foch's disciples, Colonel Louis de Grandmaison, who between 1908 and 1911 headed the War Ministry's important Operations Branch. It was reflected too in the army's superb, quick-firing 75mm field gun, which more than matched its German 77mm equivalent, although medium and heavy artillery were given a lower priority.

The plan with which the French went to war – known as Plan XVII – was prepared under the guidance of General Joseph Joffre, the Chief of the French General Staff from

1911 and the Commander-in-Chief designate in the event of hostilities. The imperturbable Joffre, a follower of the Foch–Grandmaison philosophy, rejected a previous scheme for a defensive concentration along the Belgian border and instead announced his intention to 'advance with all forces united to attack the German armies'. Five French field armies would be deployed under Plan XVII. Of these, the First and Second Armies on the right wing were to advance into Lorraine, exactly as Schlieffen had hoped. In the centre, the Third Army would attack towards Thionville and Metz. The Fifth Army, situated on the left between Mézières and Montmédy, had a more flexible role and, depending upon the route the Germans took, would either follow the Third Army's general direction or thrust north-east through the Belgian Ardennes and Luxembourg. The Fourth Army would be kept in semi-reserve, ready to reinforce the left or centre as required.

While more adaptable than the Schlieffen Plan, the French Plan XVII had a fundamental weakness. In grossly

The rival war plans

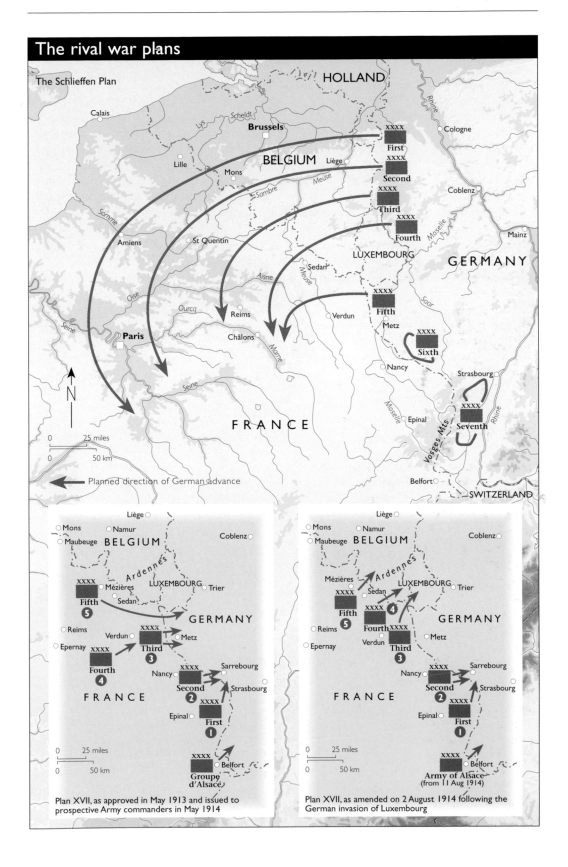

The Schlieffen Plan

Planned direction of German advance

Plan XVII, as approved in May 1913 and issued to prospective Army commanders in May 1914

Plan XVII, as amended on 2 August 1914 following the German invasion of Luxembourg

underestimating the extent to which German reserve troops would be employed alongside regular formations, the French, from the outset, were badly wrong-footed by the breadth and strength of the German sweep through Belgium. The Belgian Field Army was not expected to be a major player in the unfolding drama. Belgium had introduced conscription in 1913 but, when the crisis came, mobilised only 117,000 officers and men. The outbreak of war also found the Field Army divided by strategic disputes and in the middle of reorganisation.

Joffre also accorded relatively little weight to a possible British contribution when drawing up Plan XVII. Traditionally shielded from invasion by the Royal Navy, Britain still had a small, long-service professional army, raised by voluntary enlistment and regarded as sufficient to police and garrison her

A battery of French 75mm quick-firing field guns in action in 1914. The barrel of the gun nearest the camera is at full recoil. (IWM)

world-wide empire and protect British interests overseas. Five separate compulsory-service Bills had been placed before Parliament between 1908 and 1914 but all had been defeated. The underlying problem was that, in peacetime, no political party was prepared to risk the wrath of the taxpayer or commit electoral suicide by shedding the voluntary system and supporting a financially costly expansion of the Army. The reforms of R.B. Haldane, as Secretary of State for War from 1905 to 1912, had thus to be achieved within an agreed military budget which, during most of his term of office, was limited to around £28,000,000. Even after Haldane's reforms – and including its Regular Reserve, Special Reserve and part-time Territorial Force – the British Army, on mobilisation, only totalled some 733,000. There was the possibility of receiving reinforcements from India and the Dominions, although India's security could not be jeopardised and Dominion manpower was as yet of uncertain quantity and quality.

The principal offensive component of the Army was the British Expeditionary Force (BEF) of six infantry divisions and one cavalry division, numbering approximately 120,000. Behind this were the 'Saturday Afternoon Soldiers' of the Territorial Force, formed from the old Volunteer Force in 1908. Some 269,000 strong in July 1914, the Territorial Force had been created chiefly for home defence but could provide a framework for future Army expansion if necessary. Both the Regular Army and the Territorial Force were below establishment in 1914 and lacked heavy artillery. However, individually the men of the BEF were better trained than any of their European counterparts and had unrivalled standards of rifle-shooting, with many infantrymen capable of firing 15 aimed rounds per minute.

No agreement existed which irreversibly bound the BEF to fight on the European mainland if war came. However, Anglo-French staff talks since 1906 made this probable. As no one – least of all the Admiralty – had succeeded in putting forward a compelling and realistic alternative, the only cogent plan for the deployment of the BEF likely to be implemented, if only by default, was one that had been prepared after 1910 by the Director of Military Operations, Brigadier-General Henry Wilson, an ardent Francophile and friend of Foch. Under this scheme the BEF, on mobilisation, would assemble on the French left, in the Hirson–Maubeuge–Le Cateau area. Minimal consideration had been given to the long-term ramifications of this deployment. The logical corollaries to any meaningful continental commitment were the possible need to raise a mass army and the related necessity for industrial mobilisation to ensure that these much larger forces would be properly supplied. Britain's experiences in the first half of the coming war would be all the more painful because the country was permitted to enter a major conflict without any blueprint for military or industrial expansion or, indeed, any clear idea of the scale of effort that might be required.

Countdown to war

The incident that finally ignited the flames of war in Europe occurred on 28 June 1914, when, during an official visit to Sarajevo, capital of the newly annexed Austrian province of Bosnia, Archduke Franz Ferdinand, the heir to the Austrian throne, was assassinated with his wife. The assassin, Gavrilo Princip, was one of a group of conspirators recruited and despatched to Sarajevo by the Black Hand, a Serbian terrorist group, with the connivance of the

Archduke Franz Ferdinand leaves the City Hall, Sarajevo, on 28 June 1914, shortly before he was assassinated. (IWM)

chief of Serbian military intelligence. The Serbian government itself did not inspire the assassination but certainly knew of the plot and made well intentioned, if feeble, attempts to warn Austria about it. Austria eagerly exploited the opportunity to humble Serbia and thereby snuff out her challenge to Austro-Hungarian authority in the Balkans. First, however, Austria sought Germany's backing for her proposed course of action. Germany, in turn, saw in the Austro-Serbian confrontation a golden chance of securing hegemony in Europe, achieving world status while splitting the encircling *Entente* powers,

German troops are given a rousing send-off as they leave by train for the front, August 1914. (IWM)

forestalling Russian modernisation, eradicating the dangers to Austria-Hungary and suffocating domestic opposition. Even though it might drag the whole of Europe into armed conflict, Germany was prepared to take this calculated risk to achieve her ends. Therefore, on 5 and 6 July Germany gave Austria a 'blank cheque' of unconditional support against Serbia.

Having obtained Germany's endorsement, on 23 July Austria issued a ten-point ultimatum to Serbia. The latter accepted nine of the points but rejected, in part, the demand that Austrian officials should be involved in the investigation of the assassination, regarding such interference as a challenge to her sovereignty. On 25 July Serbia mobilised her army; Russia also confirmed partial mobilisation before entering, on 26 July, a 'period preparatory to war'. Austria reciprocated by mobilising the same day and then, on 28 July, declared war on Serbia. Up to this point it might still have been possible to isolate the problem, but Germany continued to act in an uncompromising manner which only served

to heighten tensions and gave the crisis international dimensions. On 29 July Germany demanded an immediate cessation of Russian preparations, failing which Germany would be forced to mobilise. Russia could not afford to acquiesce meekly in the destruction of Serbian sovereignty, or increased Austrian influence in eastern and south-eastern Europe. Consequently, on 30 July Russia ordered general mobilisation in support of Serbia.

Russian mobilisation began the following day but was not the inevitable precursor to war: her forces could, if necessary, have stayed on their own territory for weeks while negotiations proceeded. Germany, however, proclaimed a *Kriegsgefahrzustand* (threatening danger of war) on 31 July and presented Russia with an ultimatum. Russia's failure to respond led Germany to order general mobilisation and declare war on Russia on 1 August. This action caused France to mobilise and set in motion the remaining cogs in the intricate machinery of European alliances and understandings, for the Schlieffen Plan required, from the outset, a violation of neutral Belgium and an attack on France, quite independent of any action the Russians might take. On 2 August Germany handed Belgium an ultimatum insisting on the right of passage through her territory. This was firmly rejected and the next day Germany declared war on France.

Early on 4 August German forces crossed the frontier into Belgium. The strength of the German armies on this flank was awesome. Colonel-General Alexander von Kluck's First Army, on the extreme right, numbered 320,000 troops. The neighbouring Second Army, under Colonel-General Karl von Bülow, and the Third Army, commanded by General Max von Hausen, respectively totalled 260,000 and 180,000. The invasion

of Belgian territory brought Britain into the conflict. Though she had no formal agreements with France and Russia, Britain was committed in principle, by a treaty concluded in 1839, to guarantee Belgian independence and neutrality. In 1906 the Foreign Office had observed that this pledge did not oblige Britain to aid Belgium 'in any circumstances and at whatever risk' but, realistically, the huge threat posed by Germany to the balance of power and the Channel ports had to be resisted. Moreover, it proved much easier for Britain's Liberal Cabinet to rally the nation behind a war for 'gallant little Belgium' than behind an abstract concept such as the preservation of the status quo or the balance of power. Britain's own ultimatum expired without reply at 11pm (London time) on 4 August and she declared war on Germany.

War on the Western Front 1914–1916

The invasion of Belgium

The changes to the Schlieffen Plan wrought by Moltke dictated that the German right-wing armies must pass through the Meuse Gap between Holland and the Ardennes, a narrow corridor dominated by Liège. Failure to capture Liège and its ring of 12 forts quickly would wreck the complex German timetable at the start. A force of six brigades had the task of reducing Liège. Attached to this force was Erich Ludendorff, who as head of the General Staff's mobilisation and deployment section from 1908 to 1913 had been largely instrumental in planning the operation. The forts could withstand 21cm shells but the Skoda works at Pilsen and the Krupp works at Essen had produced huge 30.5cm and 42cm 'Big Bertha' howitzers capable of firing armour-piercing shells over seven miles.

A flawed deployment also impaired the Belgian defence. King Albert, as Commander-in-Chief, advocated a concentration on the Meuse, between Namur and Liège, so that the Belgian Army could delay the Germans further forward until Franco-British support arrived. However, the Chief of Staff, General de Selliers de Moranville, cautiously stationed most of his forces centrally behind the River Gette, where they could cover Brussels and, if necessary, fall back on Antwerp.

A German 42cm 'Big Bertha' howitzer of the type used to bombard Liège in August 1914. (IWM)

Belgian troops during the withdrawal to Antwerp, 20 August 1914. Note the dog-drawn machine guns. (IWM)

Consequently, when the crisis came King Albert barely had time to send one division to Namur and another, plus one brigade, to reinforce Liège.

The assault on 5 August began badly for the Germans. As casualties grew, Ludendorff himself assumed command of the attack in the centre. By 7 August the Germans had penetrated the ring of forts and entered Liège, where Ludendorff audaciously secured the surrender of the Citadel. The forts held out until the huge howitzers materialised on 12 August, then within four days all were battered into submission, allowing the German right-wing armies to advance. Ludendorff, now a national hero, went to the Eastern Front as Chief of Staff of General Paul von Hindenburg's Eighth Army.

The non-appearance of French and British forces persuaded the Belgian Field Army to withdraw towards Antwerp on 18 August.

Two days later the Germans entered Brussels. Bombarded by the German super-heavy howitzers, the city of Namur fell on 23 August, followed swiftly by the last of its forts. To maintain their schedule and avoid leaving substantial rearguards, the Germans implemented a policy of *Schrecklichkeit* ('frightfulness'), attempting to subdue the population by executing civilians or destroying property. Alleged civilian resistance against the rearguard of the First Army led, for example, to the burning of Louvain and its library of irreplaceable medieval manuscripts.

One can question whether the defence of Liège and subsequent resistance did much to delay the German advance. The Germans might actually have *gained* four or five days if Belgian opposition had been weaker but they still managed to cross Belgium more or less on time. What really harmed their plan was the need to detach some five corps from their right wing to invest Namur, Maubeuge and Antwerp.

Battle of the Frontiers

The French Plan XVII was first put to the test on 6 August, when Bonneau's VII Corps advanced into Upper Alsace. Bonneau was soon obliged, by German troops from Strasbourg, to retire but the Army of Alsace, under General Pau, tried again on 14 August, retaking Mulhouse. However, as threats to the Allied left and centre developed, Joffre had to withdraw Pau's formations for use elsewhere along the front. These opening moves left the French with only a small corner of Alsace in the eastern foothills of the Vosges.

The principal thrust into Lorraine by Dubail's First Army and De Castelnau's Second Army also began on 14 August. Schlieffen had intended the German left-wing armies to give ground, enticing the French forces away from the decisive right wing, but when Crown Prince Rupprecht of Bavaria proposed a counter-attack by his own Sixth Army and von Heeringen's Seventh Army, Moltke – seduced by the prospect of enveloping both French flanks – let them proceed.

The subsequent actions at Sarrebourg and Morhange on 20 August rapidly revealed that,

for the French infantry, offensive spirit would not by itself triumph over modern artillery and machine guns. The French, suffering enormous losses, were pushed back on their own frontier fortifications. Here, however, they mustered sufficient strength and resolve to organise a successful defence of Nancy and the Moselle line. The modifications to their original plan had not, in the event, enabled the Germans to deal the French right a mortal blow, and as the fighting in this region became less intense Joffre could again transfer troops to buttress the Allied centre and left. On the other hand, having vastly underestimated the extent to which the Germans would employ reservists, and still unaware of the real width of the German drive through Belgium, Joffre misjudged the strength of the German centre. On being ordered to advance north-east into the Ardennes, Ruffey's Third Army and De Langle de Cary's Fourth Army blundered into German forces around Neufchâteau and Virton on 21/22 August and were bloodily repulsed.

Soldiers of a French infantry regiment are cheered by civilians in 1914. The photograph illustrates public enthusiasm for the war at that time. (IWM)

Colonel-General Alexander von Kluck, commander of the German First Army in 1914. (IWM)

Moltke's overall handling of operations was even less certain than that of the French. On 17 August he made a misguided effort to improve the co-ordination of the German right wing, placing Kluck under the orders of the more cautious Bülow. This irritated the pugnacious Kluck and also inhibited him from swinging the First Army as far west as was necessary to turn the Allied left. Nevertheless, the true scale of German strength and movements began to dawn upon Lanrezac, the French Fifth Army commander, as he approached the Sambre and Meuse between Charleroi and Givet and found the German Second and Third Armies advancing towards him from the north and east through Belgium. His warnings caused some at French General Headquarters to brand him a defeatist, but as Bülow's forces crossed the Sambre on 21 August and French counter-attacks failed the next day, all hopes of a French offensive to the north-east evaporated. On 22 August, displaying untypical impetuosity and without waiting for Hausen's Third Army, Bülow pressed the French back an additional five miles. This counteracted the planned effect of Hausen's Meuse crossing on 23 August for, with the French Fifth Army further south than expected, it was correspondingly harder to attack its rear. Even so, when Hausen appeared on his right, Lanrezac felt that he must act immediately to avert disaster.

The Battle of Mons

By this time the BEF, under Field-Marshal Sir John French, had reached the Maubeuge–Le Cateau area, on the Allied left. Field-Marshal Lord Kitchener – who had been appointed Secretary of State for War on 5 August – feared that this forward concentration might lead to the BEF being overwhelmed by the German forces massing north of the Meuse. He could not change the assembly area but the perceived threat of a German invasion caused him to delay the embarkation of two Regular divisions. Thus at the start of the campaign the volatile Sir John French only had four infantry divisions and one cavalry division to hand. His problems, and his temper, worsened when the commander of II Corps, Grierson, suffered a fatal heart attack and Kitchener chose to replace him with General Sir Horace Smith-Dorrien, whose relations with French had long been tense. Nevertheless, after an otherwise smooth assembly, the BEF moved up into the industrial region near Mons on 22 August, expecting to participate in an Allied offensive into Belgium.

Instead it speedily became evident that the BEF was directly in the path of the German First Army sweeping down from the north-east, Lanrezac having failed to stop the Germans on the Sambre. Despite his exposed position, Sir John promised to cover Lanrezac's left by standing at Mons for,

Men of the 4th Battalion, Royal Fusiliers, resting in the Grand Place, Mons, on 23 August 1914. (IWM)

24 hours. II Corps manned the line of the Mons-Condé Canal and a small salient around the town, while Lieutenant-General Sir Douglas Haig's I Corps was to its right. For a time Kluck was ignorant of the British deployment across his axis of advance. During the morning of 23 August his leading corps – running headlong into the BEF – made a succession of piecemeal, badly co-ordinated assaults against Smith-Dorrien's positions in the salient and along the canal. The BEF's incomparable musketry exacted a terrible toll from the dense German formations but the British quickly became acquainted with the power and accuracy of the German artillery. Although Haig's I Corps was not heavily engaged, Smith-Dorrien's troops largely held on until the late afternoon, when relentless German pressure

and numerical superiority finally told. Accordingly II Corps fell back about two miles to pre-selected positions.

The BEF had performed well in its first important battle, keeping Kluck's First Army at bay for the best part of a day. Most of the 1,600 British casualties were in II Corps. That night, however, the threat to the French Fifth Army's right near Dinant prompted Lanrezac to withdraw without consulting Joffre or the British. The BEF had no alternative but to conform with Lanrezac. In some respects this proved a blessing in disguise, as the rearward move coincided with renewed German efforts to turn the vulnerable British left flank.

Allied retreat

In the last week of August, the Allied armies were everywhere in retreat, though they retained enough resilience to organise determined rearguard operations. It was at this point, with Plan XVII in tatters and the truth about the German use of reservists becoming frighteningly apparent, that the impassive Joffre displayed his best qualities. Refusing to abandon all thoughts of an offensive, he created a new Sixth Army, commanded by General Maunoury, on the endangered Allied left, having coolly taken troops from his own reserves and the French right for this purpose. Joffre's calmness under pressure was in total contrast to the increasing nervousness of his opponent, Moltke. As Falkenhayn and Ludendorff would show in years to come, the German General Staff often allowed fleeting operational opportunities to obscure its original strategic aim. Moltke was no different in this regard. The dazzling prospect of achieving a double envelopment of the Allied armies had already

Colonel-General Helmuth Graf von Moltke, Chief of the German General Staff from 1906 to 1914. (IWM)

persuaded him to give the commanders of his left-wing armies their head, and on 25 August he further dismantled the Schlieffen Plan by releasing two corps from the key right wing to help block the Russian advance in East Prussia. Given that formations had also been detached to deal with various fortresses, the three German right-wing armies had by now lost more than a quarter of their strength and had still not fulfilled their principal task.

For the Allied and German troops who had to march some 20 miles a day in the searing late August heat, thirst, fatigue, hunger and blistered feet were of much greater concern than the grand designs of their commanders. After the battle of Mons, the BEF's two corps had become separated by the Forest of Mormal. On 26 August, Smith-Dorrien judged that the Germans were so close to II Corps that he could not disengage without fighting another battle. Contrary to the wishes of Sir John French, he conducted a determined holding action at Le Cateau, where the Germans again suffered severely in the face of the BEF's musketry. II Corps itself lost 7,182 officers and men, but because of its timely stand was able to continue its retreat in relatively good order.

Smith-Dorrien's strained relations with Sir John French deteriorated beyond repair after Le Cateau. However, the stand by II Corps achieved its objective, for it not only led the Germans to overestimate British strength but also deterred Kluck from immediate pursuit. Moreover, Kluck's mistaken conclusion that the BEF was falling back south-west rather than to the south gave the British formations an unexpected breathing space, permitting them to retreat comparatively unmolested over the next few days. Yet the respite did not dispel Sir John French's gloom. Feeling let down by the French and disheartened by the BEF's casualties, he now believed that he could only save the BEF by taking it out of the Allied line of battle and retiring behind the Seine. It took the personal intervention of Kitchener, in a hastily arranged visit to France on 1 September, to prevent Sir John from following this course.

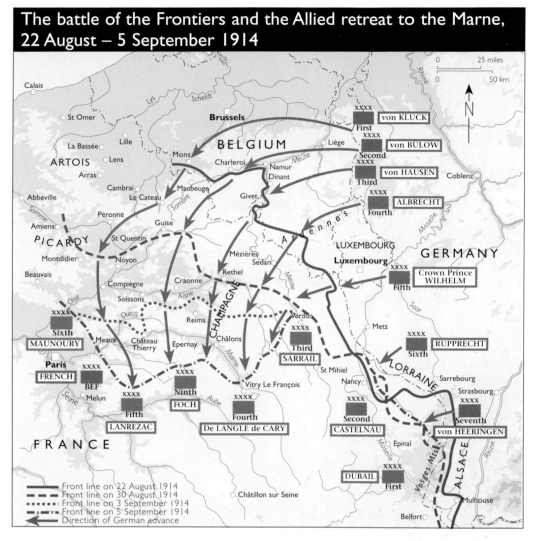

Front line on 22 August 1914
Front line on 30 August 1914
Front line on 3 September 1914
Front line on 5 September 1914
Direction of German advance

The Marne Miracle

After the BEF had escaped his clutches, Kluck was freed from Bülow's direct command on 27 August and at first headed south-west towards Amiens. By 28 August the BEF was less of a priority to him as he began to consider wheeling inwards, a move which might enable him to push Lanrezac away from Paris and to roll up the French Fifth Army's left. At this juncture Joffre ordered an unenthusiastic Lanrezac to turn his face to the west and counter-attack between Guise and St Quentin. Lanrezac, in fact, handled the operation with great skill. On 29 August, the prestigious Guard Corps of the German Second Army was

checked at Guise by the French I Corps, commanded by the energetic Franchet d'Esperey. This blow caused an apprehensive Bülow to call for Kluck's support, so presenting the latter with the pretext he required to change direction. Without seeking Moltke's prior agreement, on 30 August Kluck ordered his First Army to execute the wheel inwards. Instead of passing west of the French capital as planned, First Army would move north-east of it, exposing Kluck's flank to attack by Maunoury's French Sixth Army, now positioned north of Paris. With both events and his subordinates rapidly slipping beyond his control, Moltke tamely gave his blessing to Kluck's manoeuvre.

The glittering opportunity offered by Kluck's swerve inwards was not immediately appreciated by the Allies. One effect of the move, however, was to bring Kluck back into contact with the BEF. Some spirited rearguard actions ensued, such as that at Néry on 1 September, when 'L' Battery, Royal Horse Artillery, won three Victoria Crosses while helping to hold off the German 4th Cavalry Division for four hours. Having retreated 200 miles, the BEF crossed the Marne on 3 September but aerial reconnaissance revealed the vulnerability of Kluck's left

flank. On 4 September, as Kluck drew ahead of Bülow across the Marne, the Military Governor of Paris, General Galliéni, persuaded Joffre to halt the retreat and order the Allied left to deliver a general counter-attack. At almost the same time Moltke tacitly acknowledged the failure of the German right wing's offensive by stopping Kluck and Bülow and directing them to swing round to face the eastern side of Paris.

On 6 and 7 September Kluck coped brilliantly with the French Sixth Army's

initial attacks against his flank and communications, reversing his own First Army, pivoting to the west and sending three corps by forced marches to confront Maunoury along the Ourcq. Troops rushed from Paris in taxicabs could not prevent Maunoury's units from being pushed back, but Kluck's further movement westwards again extended the gap between the German First and Second Armies. Bülow too had responded capably to the pressure exerted by the French Fifth Army (now commanded by Franchet d'Esperey) and the newly created

Ninth Army, under Foch. By its third day the Allied counterstroke was faltering; in several places it had been repulsed with heavy losses. At the crisis of the battle, on 9 September, it was the Germans who lost their nerve. As the BEF recrossed the Marne and advanced cautiously into the gap between the two German right-wing armies, an anxious and exhausted Bülow ordered a retreat. His decision was endorsed by Lieutenant-Colonel Hentsch, a hard-working but impressionable staff officer sent to the front to represent the utterly demoralised Moltke. Kluck was left with no option but to retire northwards to the Aisne, with Bülow.

The 'Miracle of the Marne' saved Paris and dealt the final blow to German plans for a swift victory in the west. In many respects the Marne fighting had boiled down to a battle of wills between the opposing commanders. While the nerves of Moltke and Bülow had given way, the stolid Joffre had retained his grip; his reputation and his authority, as the saviour of France, would become unshakeable in the following months. Moltke, on the other hand, did not survive long in office. On 14 September General Erich von Falkenhayn was given control of operations, although to preserve appearances and morale Moltke kept his post, in name only, until 3 November. However, if the Allies had gained a momentous strategic success on the Marne, they were still a very long way from defeating the German armies.

Deadlock

Despite their reverse on the Marne, the German right-wing armies fell back to strong positions, especially the Chemin des Dames ridge, some four miles north of the River Aisne between Craonne and Soissons. Deriving is name from a road built along its crest for Louis XV's daughters, this steep, wooded ridge had a series of finger-like spurs

The 1st Battalion, The Cameronians (Scottish Rifles), cross the Marne on a pontoon bridge at La Ferté sous Jouarre, 10 September 1914. (IWM)

extending down towards the Aisne. It was here, on the BEF's line of advance, that a significant gap remained between the German First and Second Armies, but unhappily for the Allies, neither the BEF nor neighbouring French formations could push on quickly enough to exploit the situation. The BEF's commanders have since been criticised for lack of drive and unnecessary concern about their flanks, yet the troops were tired after three weeks of marching and fighting. Moreover, the BEF was advancing through countryside intersected by rivers; many bridges had been demolished by the Germans; poor weather restricted aerial reconnaissance; and a shift of front on 11 September increased congestion on roads. Upon reaching the Aisne, the BEF again found that most bridges had been destroyed and that the Germans had a considerable concentration of artillery on its northern side. Nonetheless, the bulk of the BEF's three corps – the third having been formed on 30 August – managed to cross the river on 13 September and probe forward up the valleys and spurs.

The delays cost the Allies dear, for the British were just too late in assaulting the heights north of the Aisne. The fall of Maubeuge on 7/8 September released German troops for other tasks and the VII Reserve Corps, under von Zwehl, rushed to plug the gap on the German right. Following a forced march of 40 miles in 24 hours, during which almost a quarter of its infantry dropped out, leading elements of the corps reached positions along the Chemin des Dames by 2pm on 13 September, two hours before the vanguard of Haig's I Corps, on the British right, approached the crest. Though few recognised it at the time, this was one of the defining moments of the war.

The next day, in a true 'soldier's battle' of confused, close-quarter fighting, British attempts to take the ridge met heavy artillery fire and entrenched German infantry. Some battalions of I Corps managed to pierce the German line and cross the Chemin des Dames to look down into the Ailette valley beyond. They were subsequently forced back but gallantly maintained a foothold near the crest. II and III Corps to their left had failed to make much progress, with the result that by dusk the British line stretched south-west from the Chemin des Dames on the right, down towards the Aisne near Missy and Chivres and thence westward to Crouy near Soissons. Over the following fortnight German efforts to drive the British back across the Aisne were thwarted by the BEF's superior musketry, and a defensive stand-off – dominated by machine guns, rifles and artillery – descended on the Aisne battlefield as both sides dug in. The stalemate of trench warfare had arrived on the Western Front.

Race to the sea

With deadlock gripping the front from the Aisne eastwards, each side tried to turn the other's open flank to the west and north in what became known as the 'race to the sea'. Maunoury's French Sixth Army struck first astride the Oise on 17 September but was blocked near Noyon by the German IX Reserve Corps, moving down from Antwerp. Two days later another German corps, coming from Reims, stopped an advance over the Avre by De Castelnau's Second Army, itself brought from Lorraine to bolster the Allied left. Joffre formed a new French Tenth Army, under General de Maud'huy, which attempted to get round the German right flank further north but subsequently struggled, early in October, to hold Arras against a thrust by three German corps. These operations between the Aisne and Belgium did not, however, lead to a cessation of fighting elsewhere. In late September the French beat off repeated assaults at Verdun, although the German Fifth Army, under Crown Prince Wilhelm, gained ground in the Argonne forest and a troublesome German salient was established on the western bank of the Meuse, at St Mihiel. The shape which the Western Front would largely retain until 1918 was fast being moulded.

General Erich von Falkenhayn (left) succeeded Moltke as Chief of the German General Staff. (IWM)

Worried about becoming enmeshed in the Aisne stalemate, Sir John French urged Joffre to allow the BEF to disengage and resume its former position on the Allied left. Tactically the BEF – lacking heavy artillery but possessing effective cavalry – would be of greater value on the open left flank while, strategically, it seemed sensible to shorten its lines of communication with the Channel ports. Despite the problems which would arise from the passage of British divisions across French lines of communication, Joffre sanctioned the move. On 1 October the BEF began a side-step to the Flanders plain, a region which would become one of its main fields of sacrifice for the remainder of the conflict.

In the first three weeks of October Smith-Dorrien's II Corps pushed towards La Bassée while, to the north, Major-General Pulteney's III Corps advanced towards Lille. The Cavalry Corps, commanded by Lieutenant-General Edmund Allenby and operating on Pulteney's left, occupied

Messines and Wytschaete, linking with the recently formed IV Corps which, after the surrender of Antwerp, was ordered to Ypres. The co-ordination of operations between the Oise and the sea was entrusted by Joffre to Foch, who was appointed to head a new Northern Army Group. There were no formal arrangements for unity of command and Foch had no direct powers over the British and Belgians, but in practice his allies – wherever possible – acted upon his proposals rapidly and without friction at this stage of the war.

Such co-operation was essential, for Falkenhayn was currently displaying a deft strategic touch, using railways cleverly to gain a vital edge in redeploying and reinforcing his armies. With the Germans setting the pace, the Allies were at greater risk of being outflanked in late October and early November. The German Sixth Army, which had moved across the front from Lorraine, strove to dislodge the Allies from their positions between La Bassée and Menin, and a reconstituted Fourth Army, under Duke Albrecht of Württemberg, closed in on Ypres. The latter formation included four new reserve corps with a large proportion of highly motivated young volunteers from universities and technical colleges who, although hurriedly trained, offered Falkenhayn a potentially decisive advantage as he sought to outflank the Allied left and drive down the Channel coast.

Antwerp falls

Once the 'race to the sea' gathered speed, the Germans knew that they must finally deal with the problem posed by Antwerp, to which the Belgian Field Army had withdrawn in August. The Belgians had made sorties from Antwerp on 24 August and 9 September, trying to disrupt German communications, but these efforts had merely exacerbated the exhaustion and low morale of their own troops. King Albert's objections notwithstanding, Joffre spurred him into ordering a third sortie. This had hardly begun when, on 28 September, the Germans opened a bombardment against Antwerp's outer forts.

The Germans had few spare formations available and the force they assembled, under General von Beseler, mostly comprised Reserve, *Landwehr* or *Ersatz* units. However, the 80,000 garrison troops supplementing the Belgian Field Army were of indifferent quality and Antwerp's 48 forts and redoubts were obsolete and outgunned. Hence, although numerical weakness restricted von Beseler to an assault on the city's south-eastern defences, five days of infantry attacks and bombardment by super-heavy siege artillery were enough to breach the outer ring of forts.

The Belgians were now convinced of the need to evacuate Antwerp. Warned of their intentions by the British Minister in Belgium, the British government belatedly intervened. In a personal visit to Antwerp on 3 October the First Lord of the Admiralty, Winston Churchill, persuaded the Belgians to continue their resistance provided that, within three days, the British could guarantee that relief forces would be sent. The French offered the 87th Territorial Division and a Marine Brigade while the British promised a contingent, commanded by Lieutenant-General Sir Henry Rawlinson, which contained the Regular 7th Division and 3rd Cavalry Division.

In actuality the only reinforcements to arrive were from the newly formed Royal Naval Division, which reached Antwerp between 4 and 6 October. Their presence did not prevent the Germans from extending a bridgehead across the River Nethe, thereby hastening the city's fall.

The greater part of the Belgian Field Army duly carried out a further retirement to the Nieuport–Dixmude line along the River Yser. Rearguards, including the Royal Naval Division, left Antwerp during the night of 8/9 October and on 10 October the city formally surrendered. Rawlinson's force, designated IV Corps, had landed at Zeebrugge and Ostend but could do no more than concentrate at Ghent to cover the

withdrawal of the Royal Naval Division and Belgians before moving south-west to join the French 87th Division in protecting Ypres. The eleventh-hour British contribution to Antwerp's defence had been too small to save the city; however, it did help to delay the surrender for some five days, winning precious time for the main BEF to reach Flanders. The true value of British intervention at Antwerp, within the wider context of the whole 1914 campaign, would become clear over the next six weeks.

Fighting on the Yser

Having abandoned Antwerp, the Belgian Field Army, with the French Marine Brigade, consolidated its positions between Dixmude and the coast near Nieuport. King Albert's decision to stand there, rather than help his allies inland, proved sensible. On 14 October Falkenhayn ordered the German Sixth Army to remain temporarily on the defensive south of Ypres while the Fourth Army – incorporating the four Reserve Corps of young volunteers – made the potentially decisive thrust between Menin and the sea, towards Calais. Its right, on the coast, would be covered by von Beseler's III Reserve Corps, including units from the Antwerp operations.

Von Beseler's attack on 18 October – augmented the following day by XXII Reserve Corps – pushed back Belgian outposts east of the Yser, but further assaults on 19/20 October were repulsed at Dixmude and at Nieuport, where the Germans were shelled by Allied warships. Foch sent the French 42nd Division to stiffen the Nieuport sector, but on 22 October the Germans established a bridgehead across the Yser, at Tervaete. Once again employing their super-heavy guns, the Germans delivered repeated blows at Dixmude – now perilously close to being outflanked. As their losses grew it became progressively more difficult for the Belgians to continue their stubborn defence. Consequently, on 28 October they opened the gates of the Furnes lock at Nieuport and flooded the low ground east of the embankment carrying the Nieuport–Dixmude railway.

At first this desperate measure did not stop the Germans who, by noon on 30 October, had seized Ramscapelle and reached Pervyse. However, that night the rising water forced von Beseler to pull III Reserve Corps back across the Yser, followed, two days later, by XXII Reserve Corps. Frustrated near the coast, Falkenhayn and Duke Albrecht were obliged to turn their attention inland again and launch their next major attack in the Ypres area.

The first battle of Ypres

While the struggle on the Yser raged, the BEF had largely clung to its positions at Messines, Ploegsteert and La Bassée. The farmland surrounding the Belgian town of Ypres was now the only sector where either side had a real chance of outflanking the enemy. Arriving from the Aisne on 20 October,

Haig's I Corps advanced north of Ypres, near Langemarck, but ran head-on into the German XXIV and XXVI Reserve Corps approaching from the north-east. Far from striking a decisive blow, the Allies became embroiled in a fluctuating encounter battle during which they were compelled to feed in units piecemeal simply to hold their ground. On the German side, the patriotism of the young volunteers could not disguise their limited training and they fell in thousands at Langemarck, attacking in dense skirmish lines. Remembered by the Germans as the *Kindermord von Ypern* (Massacre of the Innocents at Ypres), their sacrifice was later accorded a special place in Nazi mythology.

Although the front remained fluid, trenches were now snaking across the flat farmland. Aware, by the evening of 24 October, that the Reserve Corps assaults

The 2nd Battalion, Royal Scots Fusiliers, digging trenches north of the Menin Road, near Ypres, 20 October 1914. (IWM)

The first battle of Ypres, October–November 1914

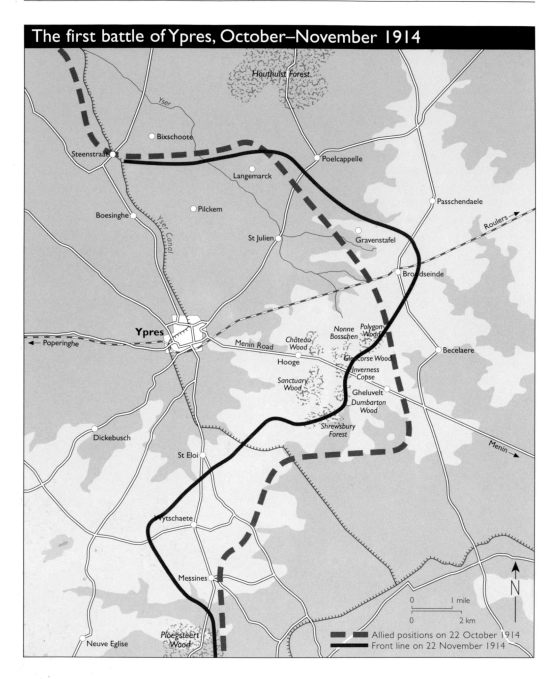

Allied positions on 22 October 1914
Front line on 22 November 1914

would probably fail, the Germans decided to make a fresh attack a few miles further south, between Gheluvelt and Messines. There, on 29 October, a task force under General von Fabeck renewed German efforts to achieve a breakthrough. The Allies experienced a major crisis on 31 October when the British positions at Gheluvelt were overrun but, as at Langemarck, the Germans

lost cohesion after the initial breach, again exposing weaknesses in their training, and a bold counterattack by 357 officers and men of the 2nd Worcestershires drove them from Gheluvelt.

Over the next few days, however, Allenby's cavalry and the French were pushed off Messines Ridge. The situation was stabilised with the deployment of extra French troops on the BEF's flanks but the respite was brief. Another German assault on 11 November saw a composite Prussian Guard Division break through the British lines just north of the Menin Road. Once more employing obsolete tightly packed formations, the Germans were halted by a combination of point-blank British artillery fire and a scratch force which included cooks, brigade headquarters clerks and engineers. Not knowing that this represented the last line of British resistance, the Prussian Guard faltered and were then cleared from the *Nonne Bosschen* (Nun's Wood) by a vigorous counter-attack by the 2nd Oxfordshire and Buckinghamshire Light Infantry.

The Allies had survived the last crisis of 1914. Within a week or so snow cloaked the battlefield and the grandiose plans of the belligerents lay in ruins. The transfer of four German cavalry and eight infantry divisions

to the Eastern Front by early December underlined Falkenhayn's acknowledgement of that fact. Despite gaining a great deal of valuable territory in Belgium and northern France, the Germans now faced their ultimate nightmare: a prolonged two-front war, the very scenario they had sought to avoid. The original, highly trained, professional BEF had also gone beyond recall. It had done much to halt the German drive on the Channel ports but suffered 58,000 additional casualties between 14 October and 30 November. The forces of the British Empire had begun their long and bloody association with Ypres, where the Allies occupied a hazardous salient dominated by German-held ridges to the south and east.

The Cloth Hall at Ypres, showing the damage caused by German artillery fire in October and November 1914. (IWM)

The Winter of 1914–1915

With the onset of winter, the deadlock became total. Continuous trench lines now extended from the Belgian coast to the Swiss frontier. The Germans had not yet constructed the formidable defensive systems which, for most of the war, their overall strategy in the west would dictate. Believing, in late 1914, that the building of a second position might weaken the resolve of troops in the front defences, the Germans depended at first on a single line, to be held at all costs. However, during the winter they revised this

Field-Marshal Sir John French, Commander-in-Chief of the British Expeditionary Force, August 1914 to December 1915. (IWM)

policy, adding depth to these defences with concrete machine-gun posts 1,000 yards to the rear of the front line. The 21 miles of front then held by the BEF, between Wytschaete and the La Bassée Canal, ran through the low-lying Flanders plain, where the shallow trenches often flooded.

Having prepared for siege operations at the outset of the war, the Germans were comparatively well endowed with weapons suitable for trench warfare, including mortars, grenades, heavy guns and

Soldiers of the 2nd Royal Scots Fusiliers in a rudimentary trench near Neuve Chapelle during the winter of 1914–15. (IWM)

howitzers. The BEF, however, was compelled to fashion improvised mortars from drainpipes and grenades from jam tins. All the armies were experiencing shell shortages. Falkenhayn later stated that the failure of just one ammunition train that winter 'threatened to render whole sections of the front defenceless'. The French, requiring 50,000 rounds of 75mm ammunition daily, were producing only 11,000 rounds per day in mid-November 1914, while by January some British 18-pounder guns were restricted to firing just four rounds a day. Steps were taken at home to increase munitions production, but British industry could not be transformed overnight to meet the war's unprecedented demands.

Casualty rates in 1914 hit the BEF particularly hard. As a small, professional volunteer force it could ill afford the loss of

Men of the London Rifle Brigade fraternise with Saxon troops, near Ploegsteert, Christmas 1914. (IWM)

3,627 officers and 86,237 men between August and December 1914, most casualties being among the Regulars of its first seven divisions. To compensate for the losses, the Indian Corps reached the Western Front in October, followed, between November and January, by the 8th, 27th and 28th Divisions – all formed from Regulars drawn from overseas garrisons. Twenty-three Territorial battalions also reinforced the BEF in 1914, and in February the 1st Canadian Division arrived. On 26 December the BEF was reorganised into two Armies: the First Army

under Haig and the Second Army under Smith-Dorrien. In Britain, Kitchener, who foresaw a long and costly war, had begun a vast expansion of Britain's military forces, forming a series of 'New Armies', each of which duplicated the six divisions of the original BEF. More than 1,186,000 volunteers enlisted in the first five months, but they would take time to train.

Meanwhile the British soldiers at the front were struggling to hold the line. Musketry standards had already declined and morale had slumped as the Germans made gains in minor operations at Givenchy in December and near Cuinchy in January. Christmas 1914 was marked by a spontaneous unofficial truce in Flanders, where German and British soldiers fraternised in No Man's Land, taking photographs, swapping souvenirs and even playing football. Hardening attitudes, as the war became increasingly bloody and impersonal, ensured that such incidents on this scale would not recur, but 'live and let live' understandings – accepted by both sides – frequently prevailed in quiet sectors until the Armistice.

Falkenhayn's decision in November 1914 to stand temporarily on the defensive in the west – where he believed the war would ultimately be won – proved a huge mistake. A weakened and now inexperienced BEF might not have withstood further heavy blows during the winter, but the respite granted by the Germans allowed the Allies to reorganise, giving Britain, in particular, the chance to train Kitchener's New Armies and strengthen the BEF with additional Territorial and Dominion contingents. Falkenhayn hoped that once the Russians had been pushed back over the Vistula he would resume the offensive in the west. However, a combination of factors forced him to continue with a predominantly defensive strategy there in 1915.

Austria needed a major victory to deter neighbouring Romania and Italy from joining the Allies, and without extra German assistance, especially in the Carpathians, it was feared that Austria might even seek a separate peace. Hindenburg and Ludendorff could claim that all the titanic efforts in the west had resulted only in deadlock, whereas they – with fewer resources – had twice frustrated Russian attempts to invade Germany and had also won territory in Russian Poland. Since both the Kaiser and his Chancellor, Bethmann-Hollweg, agreed that the Eastern Front should be given priority, Falkenhayn found it necessary to stifle his own immediate strategic inclinations.

For the French the options were far simpler. The Germans occupied large areas of Belgium and northern France – including regions rich in raw materials or heavy industry. These could only be liberated through an offensive policy. Joffre remained convinced that a breakthrough was possible, but conceded that a succession of preliminary attacks might be required to devour German reserves before the enemy line finally ruptured. In a phrase attributed to Joffre – *Je les grignote* ('I keep nibbling at them') – lay the embryo of three years of attrition. But where should the French strike? Joffre decided to pinch out the German-held salient between Reims and Arras, the snout of which, at Noyon, pointed towards Paris. He would attack it from two directions. One thrust eastwards, from Artois, might drive the Germans back across the Douai plain and menace their supply lines to Cambrai and St Quentin, while another advance northwards, from Champagne, could sever railway links feeding the German centre. A third offensive, launched from the Verdun–Nancy front, might also cut the Thionville–Hirson railway communications and loosen the German grip in this sector, as the routes north of the Ardennes could not, by themselves, sustain the whole German front in the west.

'Papa' Joffre, the French Commander-in-Chief, 1914–1916.

Joffre's strategy, which shaped Franco-British operations throughout 1915, was essentially sound. In an amended form it would produce decisive results in the second half of 1918. However, during the war's first winter, the Allies had neither the means nor the tactical skills to apply it successfully and, lacking appropriate equipment and fresh troops, Joffre could only mount significant attacks on the fronts of the Fourth Army in Champagne and the Tenth Army in Artois.

Directed by Foch, the left-hand blow of Joffre's winter offensives was struck on 17 December in Artois. De Maud'huy's Tenth Army attempted to pierce the German defences around Souchez, north of Arras, and seize Vimy Ridge, which offered excellent observation over the Lens coalfield and the Douai plain. Pétain's XXXIII Corps was ordered to secure Carency, guarding the western approaches to Souchez, and Maistre's XXI Corps would press towards the Notre Dame de Lorette spur, situated on the other side of the Souchez valley, opposite the north-western end of Vimy Ridge. Since they were short of heavy artillery, the French had to stagger their attacks, allowing the Germans to concentrate their defensive firepower. Fog, rain and thick mud hampered operations and forced the French to end the Artois attacks early in January 1915; they had incurred nearly 8,000 casualties for meagre gains on the southern edge of Carency and north of Notre Dame de Lorette.

On 20 December the Fourth Army had attacked on a 20-mile front in Champagne. The XVII and Colonial Corps, on the right, achieved early successes, taking important strongpoints in the enemy front line, but XXII Corps, on the left, made little headway against flanking machine-gun fire.

Operations ran on into January, when, as in Artois, miserable weather and the exhaustion of the troops forced the French to suspend the offensive. The Germans exploited this lull to strengthen their support positions where the front line had been breached or imperilled. The second phase of this battle began on 16 February and lasted until 17 March, with limited attacks

continuing for another fortnight. The Germans experienced the full horrors of rapid 'drum fire' from French 75mm guns yet only yielded a few scattered villages on the forward slopes of the hills. The Champagne offensive cost the French some 240,000 casualties and failed to disrupt the railway communications supplying the German centre.

Diversionary attacks in support of the main offensives did not alleviate the gloom. On the Aisne, ground was won by Maunoury's Sixth Army at Vauxrot and Crouy, but the French were pushed back to the left bank in January by a brutal German counterstroke. Assaults by Sarrail's Third Army between the Meuse and Argonne, intended to cover the right of the Champagne offensive, led to a further 12,000 French casualties. The eastern flank bore witness to a savage struggle for the Hartmannsweilerkopf. This peak, dominating the Alsace plain, was in French possession by 26 April, though the Army of the Vosges (later the French Seventh Army) lost 20,000 men in the four-month battle.

Despite Joffre's assurances in March 1915 that French soldiers had 'an obvious superiority in morale', his winter offensives had been expensive failures. Given his previous service as an engineer officer, his inability to adapt to what were basically siege warfare conditions was as disappointing as his want of tactical flair. Even Foch, the arch-apostle of *élan*, reviewed his tactical principles as the need for sufficient heavy artillery to destroy enemy trenches and strongpoints became increasingly apparent.

Neuve Chapelle

The BEF, after a wretched winter in the trenches, was in no state to support the French offensives until the early spring of 1915. However, knowing that the War Council in London was considering operations in the Dardanelles and Balkans, its senior commanders feared that unless the BEF made a positive contribution soon, resources might be diverted away from the Western Front. The appointment of Lieutenant-General Sir William Robertson as the BEF's Chief of Staff in January also brought a more robust approach to the work of General Headquarters (GHQ). By mid-February a plan was approved for an attack by Haig's First Army on a narrow, 2,000-yard front in Flanders. The aim was to eliminate the German salient around Neuve Chapelle, secure Aubers Ridge and threaten Lille, an important road and rail junction. The despatch of the Regular 29th Division to the Dardanelles prevented the BEF from relieving the French IX Corps at Ypres and precluded a simultaneous French attack in Artois. Rather than postpone Haig's operation indefinitely, Sir John French decided that it should go ahead independently, if only to demonstrate that the BEF could do more than merely hold the line.

The First Army's thorough planning provided the BEF with a valuable template for future set-piece trench assaults. Photographic reconnaissance by the Royal Flying Corps facilitated the production and distribution of detailed trench maps and enabled the assaulting units to rehearse the initial phase of the attack, while precise artillery timetables were issued for the first time. The artillery was allocated 100,000 rounds – one-sixth of the BEF's total stocks – and was limited to a 35-minute hurricane bombardment, following which fire would be lifted from the enemy front trenches and a barrage laid down to impede German reinforcements.

On 10 March, the day of the assault, the surprised German defenders were numbed by the hurricane bombardment. The attacking brigades of the Indian Corps and Rawlinson's IV Corps swiftly took the front trenches. Thereafter delays on the flanks caused congestion in the centre, and German strongpoints also held up the advance – robbing the attack of its impetus. British and Indian troops had seized the German defences on a frontage of 4,000 yards, penetrated to a maximum depth of 1,200 yards, captured Neuve Chapelle and

Neuve Chapelle village after its capture by the British 8th Division, March 1915. (IWM)

flattened the salient west of the village, but they could not exploit their early gains. Haig therefore suspended the attack late on 12 March. The British had suffered nearly 13,000 casualties, the Germans about 12,000. The BEF could now be taken seriously as an attacking force, yet Neuve Chapelle also highlighted several intrinsic problems of

trench assaults. Careful preparation would generally help attackers to break into enemy positions but it was much harder to move artillery and reserves forward quickly enough to *break out* of those defences before enemy reinforcements arrived. The absence of adequate means of communication also rendered it extremely difficult for

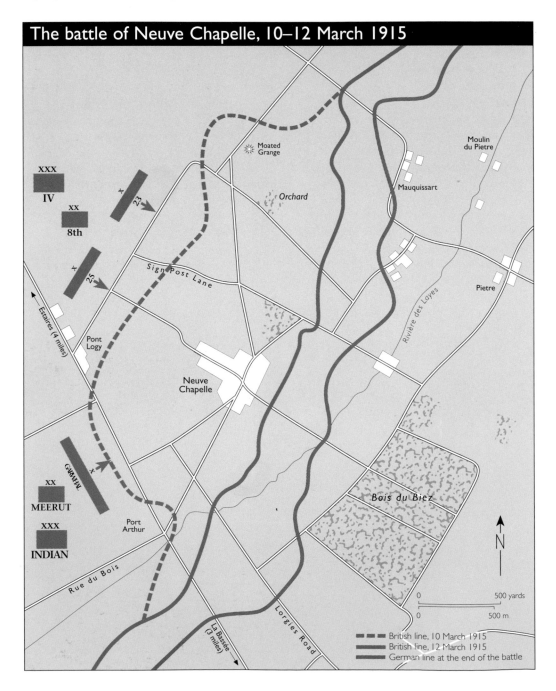

The battle of Neuve Chapelle, 10–12 March 1915

■ ■ ■ ■ British line, 10 March 1915
▬▬▬▬ British line, 12 March 1915
▬▬▬▬ German line at the end of the battle

commanders to control operations once shells had destroyed forward telephone cables and runners had been killed or wounded. However, the effectiveness of the short hurricane bombardment was one lesson which the BEF, to its cost, largely ignored or discounted over the next two years.

The second battle of Ypres

Before the Allies could launch their next offensive operations the Germans – employing poison gas for the first time on the Western Front – attacked the northern flank of the Ypres Salient. This blow reflected all the confusion of strategic purpose that characterised Falkenhayn's term as Chief of the German General Staff. The Salient was important to both sides, but because Falkenhayn still accorded priority to the Eastern Front, the use of gas at Ypres was largely experimental. Thus the objectives of XXIII and XXVI Reserve Corps were confined to Langemarck, Pilckem Ridge and the Yser canal line up to Ypres itself, while the Fourth Army was denied fresh reserves. However, the Germans hoped that the capture of the higher ground near Pilckem might render it impossible for the Allies to hold the Salient.

The French 45th (Algerian) and 87th Territorial Divisions occupied the sector between the Yser canal and Poelcappelle which the Germans were to attack. Just after 5pm on 22 April, following a short but ferocious bombardment, the Germans released clouds of chlorine gas from 5,730 cylinders. With no protection against the gas, the French divisions retreated in panic, opening a five-mile gap to the left of the 1st Canadian Division's positions. Langemarck and Pilckem fell and at dusk the Germans were only two miles from Ypres. Fortunately for the Allies, the German troops were unwilling to pursue the gas too closely and, lacking reserves, failed to grasp their sole opportunity to effect a breakthrough in the west that year. During the night a new defensive line was patched together by the British and Canadians. When a second gas attack came at St Julien on 24 April, the Canadians – using towels, bandages and handkerchiefs soaked in urine or water as

Oxygen is given to a gassed soldier at a field ambulance station at Hazebrouck in June 1915. (IWM)

improvised respirators – courageously prevented further erosion of the front.

Foch, co-ordinating Allied operations in Flanders, did not enjoy his finest hour at Ypres in April-May 1915. However, his faith in the infallibility of the offensive unshaken, and ignoring the loss of guns during the German advance, he ordered the local French commander to undertake counter-attacks which were plainly impractical. Various assaults by the BEF between 23 and 26 April, made with inadequate artillery support and negligible French assistance, failed to regain the lost ground. On 27 April, painfully aware that German gunners could now shell the Salient from the left rear, Smith-Dorrien urged withdrawal to a more defensible 'GHQ Line' to the east of Potijze and Wieltje and within 2,000 yards of Ypres. The suggestion was rejected by the mercurial Sir John French, who was in optimistic mood following a promise of extra divisions from Foch. With his doubts about Smith-Dorrien re-awakened, French immediately transferred responsibility for all British troops around Ypres to the V Corps commander, Herbert Plumer.

This incident precipitated Smith-Dorrien's resignation and he was succeeded in command of Second Army by Plumer on 6 May. The loss of the able Smith-Dorrien did not ultimately prove as calamitous to the BEF as it might have done, since Plumer displayed an almost unrivalled understanding and mastery of the new tactical conditions on the Western Front, particularly at Ypres. It is ironic that between 1 and 3 May, when the demands of the imminent Artois offensive ended hopes of French reserves being sent to Ypres, Plumer was permitted to draw back his forces, much as Smith-Dorrien had proposed, though – partly to allow room for possible future movements – Plumer's line was slightly further east, about three miles from Ypres.

In May the Germans made four more gas attacks, seizing additional ground on the Bellewaarde and Frezenberg ridges. When the battle ended, on 25 May, the Ypres Salient – now less than three miles deep – had

assumed the basic form it would keep for the next two years. For the second time in seven months the BEF had halted a German drive on Ypres; this latest defence had cost another 58,000 casualties, compared with nearly 38,000 German losses. Furthermore, with the Germans positioned on three sides and holding the key ridges to the east and south, there was no relief from the enemy guns and no foreseeable end to the suffering of BEF units occupying the Salient.

Artois and Flanders

Events on the Eastern Front, where the Central Powers had launched a devastating offensive between Gorlice and Tarnow on 2 May, made the projected Allied spring offensive in Artois even more significant as a means of giving indirect help to the Russians (See Osprey Essential Histories, *The First World War: The Eastern Front 1914–1918*, by Geoffrey Jukes). Joffre and Foch proposed that in Artois, after a prodigious six-day preliminary bombardment by 1,252 guns, the French Tenth Army, now commanded by General d'Urbal, would assault Vimy Ridge to open the way for an advance into the Douai plain.

When the offensive began, on 9 May, Pétain's XXXIII Corps – attacking in the crucial central sector – achieved early successes beyond expectations. In 90 minutes his troops moved forward two-and-a-half miles on a four-mile front and the 77th and Moroccan Divisions reached the crest of Vimy Ridge between Souchez and La Folie Farm. The drawback was that because d'Urbal had not anticipated such a swift advance, his nearest reserves were over seven miles away and could not be brought up in time to exploit these successes. Inevitably, by nightfall the Germans had counter-attacked and pushed Pétain's troops off the crest. From now on, the offensive degenerated into a bitter close-quarter struggle in the labyrinth of German strongpoints and trenches on or below the ridge. As the grisly spectre of

French troops on the Notre Dame de Lorette heights, near Souchez, in the spring of 1915. (IWM)

attrition re-imposed itself, the French made a few extra gains, securing much of the vital neighbouring spur of Notre Dame de Lorette. On 16 June the impressive Moroccan Division again reached the top of Vimy Ridge, but as before could not hold on to all its gains. Five weeks of fighting had cost an additional 100,000 French casualties while German losses totalled some 60,000. All that Joffre and Foch could show for this sacrifice was the recapture of five more miles of French soil and a precarious toe-hold on Vimy Ridge.

The BEF's part in the offensive operations of 9 May was a larger-scale version of its own March assault, with Haig's First Army attacking either side of Neuve Chapelle in a fresh effort to secure Aubers Ridge. The success of the short bombardment in March was borne in mind, but the BEF's worrying shortage of heavy guns and ammunition limited the preliminary bombardment to 45 minutes. As the German defences in this sector had been strengthened since March, the bombardment was simply not heavy enough. With plenty of time to emerge from their dug-outs and man their trench parapets relatively unscathed, the defenders inflicted 11,000 casualties for only tiny British gains, compelling Haig to terminate the attack early on 10 May.

Bowing to Joffre's calls to maintain the pressure, Sir John French approved a further First Army attack for 15 May at Festubert, about two miles north of the La Bassée Canal. A notable shift towards an attrition policy was signalled by GHQ's guidance to Haig that the enemy should be relentlessly 'worn down by exhaustion and loss until his defence collapses'. The preceding bombardment, lasting 60 hours, had been much longer than on 9 May and the objective line was deliberately less ambitious, being only 1,000 yards away. Between 15 and 27 May the BEF incurred 16,000 casualties for a maximum advance of some 1,300 yards – just enough to encourage

future reliance on longer artillery
bombardments before infantry attacks. In
coming to believe that wearing-out fights,
longer and heavier bombardments and wider
attack frontages would be needed for any
breakthrough, the French and British alike
had drawn several misleading conclusions
from the May battles and would then follow
a series of costly and false tactical trails over
the next two years.

Of much greater long-term significance,
however, was the fact that the 'Shells
Scandal' – generated in Britain by disclosures
of ammunition shortages at Aubers Ridge –
contributed directly to the creation of a
Ministry of Munitions and to the formation
of a coalition Government. The new
systematic policy of munitions production
was far better tailored to the demands of
modern war, even though the real benefits of
this were not fully evident until mid-1917.

During the spring and summer of 1915 the
expansion of the BEF gained impetus. From
February to September the BEF was augmented
by 15 New Army and six Territorial divisions.
The 2nd Canadian Division also arrived in
September, permitting the formation of the
Canadian Corps. As its strength grew, the BEF
took over more of the Allied line, including a
five-mile stretch between the La Bassée Canal
and Lens in May and an additional 15 miles
on the Somme in August. The latter sector
became the responsibility of a new Third
Army, under General Sir Charles Monro. In
June the French created three Army Groups –
the Northern, Central and Eastern –
commanded respectively by Foch,
De Castelnau and Dubail. Pétain's efforts in
Artois were rewarded by promotion to the
command of the French Second Army.

Even when no big offensives were in
prospect, the Western Front was by no means
quiet. In April the French made an abortive
attempt to eradicate the potential threat
posed to the eastern flank of Verdun by the
German-held St Mihiel salient, incurring
64,000 casualties in the process. Another

32,000 French officers and men fell in the
Argonne sector from 20 June to 14 July.
Meanwhile the Germans continued to
experiment with new weapons. After first
using flamethrowers near Verdun in February,

A shell explodes close to British troops at Y Wood near
Hooge, in the Ypres Salient, 16 June 1915. (IWM)

they subjected the raw British 14th (Light) Division to a terrifying 'liquid fire' attack at Hooge, near Ypres, on 30 July. In this sector, the short distance between the opposing trenches favoured the employment of flamethrowers; henceforth such conditions would rarely recur. Moreover, the British 6th Division, in a well-prepared minor attack on 9 August, recovered all the ground they had lost at Hooge a few days earlier.

Allied plans for the autumn

Early in June Joffre revealed his plans for a combined autumn offensive. Like those of the previous winter, they envisaged convergent attacks from Artois and Champagne to isolate and eliminate the German-held Noyon salient and its communications. Initially Joffre intended to make the principal effort in Artois, but later he decided to shift the main weight of the offensive to Champagne, where the French Second and Fourth Armies would face fewer fortified villages than the Tenth Army did in Artois. The latter would again assault Vimy Ridge supported, north of Lens, by the British.

Both Sir John French and Haig, keenly aware of their weaknesses in heavy artillery, were unhappy about the role assigned to the BEF. In particular, the First Army was expected to advance across a difficult area of villages, mines and slag heaps – precisely the sort of terrain that had persuaded Joffre to switch the main blow from Artois to Champagne. Throughout June and July Joffre and Foch refused to be swayed by the protests of the British commanders. Then, in mid-August, the deteriorating strategic situation – following Allied setbacks in Italy and Gallipoli and on the Eastern Front – prompted Kitchener to modify his own views and order French and Haig to accept Joffre's plan, 'even though by so doing we may suffer very heavy losses'.

To deliver the principal blow in the more thinly populated Champagne region, the French had to construct additional light railways and roads, causing the postponement of the offensive until 25 September. The Germans, however, were not idle and hastened to build a new second defensive position two to four miles behind the first, employing prisoners of war and French civilians to speed up the work. Despite a series of alarmist reports from the German Third Army commander, von Einem, concerning French preparations in Champagne, Falkenhayn remained sufficiently unruffled to undertake a tour of the front with the Kaiser as late as 21 September. Joffre was similarly optimistic. 'Your *élan* will be irresistible,' he assured his troops on the eve of the offensive.

The second battle of Champagne

The autumn offensive in Champagne began in a downpour on 25 September. Advancing with colours held aloft and bands playing the *Marseillaise*, the infantry of De Castelnau's Central Army Group made heartening initial progress. The German front trenches were badly damaged and their defensive barbed wire had been cut in many places by the four-day preliminary bombardment; this helped the French infantry arrive at the enemy first position in reasonably good order. They broke through in four places. Although the Moroccan Division was halted around the heights of the Bois de Perthes, in the centre of the 20-division attack frontage, the 10th Colonial Division, on its left, penetrated up to 3,000 yards in under 60 minutes and reached the German second position. To the right of the Moroccans, the 28th Division was similarly successful, and ground was also won on the extreme flanks, but most of the assaulting divisions of the French Second and Fourth Armies failed to match the gains near the Bois de Perthes.

At noon Falkenhayn – still touring the front – reached the German Fifth Army headquarters and was briefed on the situation. He reacted by switching a division from the Vosges to the German Third Army and directed units of X Corps, recently transferred from the Eastern Front, towards von Einem's battle area. The early French successes encouraged Joffre to give the Central Army Group two extra reserve divisions and to order the Eastern Army Group to pass on to it as much 75mm ammunition as could be spared. In fact, the German positions in Champagne were not seriously threatened. Having clearly seen the preparations for the offensive, the Germans had withdrawn most of their artillery behind their second position where, protected by relatively uncut wire, they intended to base their main defence.

Closing up to the German second position along a front of about eight miles on 26 September, the French won only a shallow foothold in the defences and the offensive lost momentum. The French artillery lacked direct observation over the next series of German trenches, which were sited on reverse slopes. From 27 to 29 September a succession of desperate French attacks secured just a few small lodgements in the second position. As ammunition ran low and casualties grew, Pétain, commanding the French Second Army, had the moral courage to halt operations on his own initiative, obliging Joffre, in turn, to stop the offensive. A resumption of attacks on 6 October had no better outcome. The Champagne offensive had obviously fallen short of Joffre's promises, and since French losses were nearly 144,000 – as against 85,000 German casualties – its slender gains could scarcely be justified, even by the grim standards of a long-term policy of attrition.

Loos

Haig's fears about the shortage of heavy artillery for his First Army's part in the Artois offensive were eased by the distribution of around 5,000 cylinders of chlorine gas to Lieutenant-General Hubert Gough's I Corps and Rawlinson's IV Corps. Rawlinson advocated 'bite and hold' tactics, drawing the Germans into expensive counterattacks, but Haig – visualising the possibility of something more than a subsidiary success – hoped to break through the German first and second positions between Loos and Haisnes, then advance east to the Haute Deule Canal. To this end Haig would deploy all six divisions of I and IV Corps in the main assault, on the understanding that XI Corps, in general reserve, would be transferred to him as soon as it was needed. Sir John French, who remained nervous about the coming operations, wanted to

Clouds of gas and bursting shells are visible in this photograph of the British attack on the Hohenzollern Redoubt, 13 October 1915. (IWM)

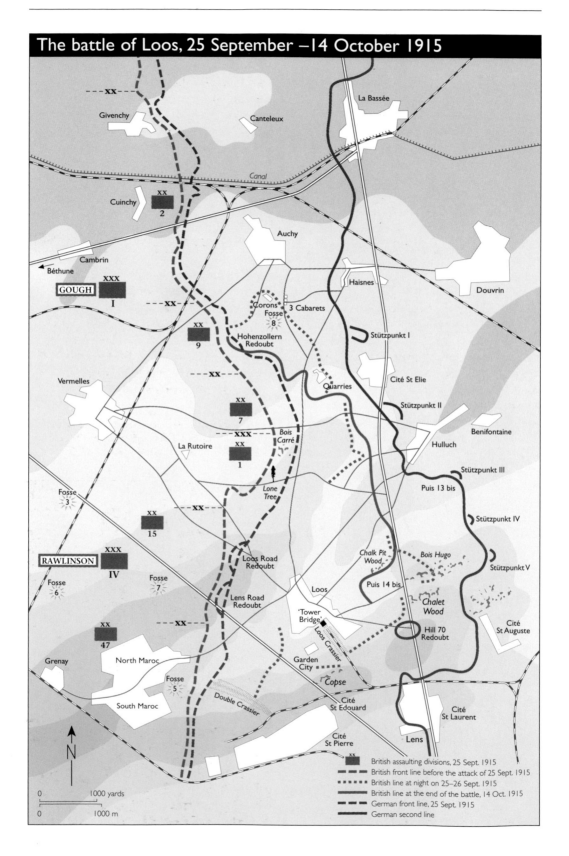

The battle of Loos, 25 September –14 October 1915

La Bassée

Givenchy

Canteleux

Canal

Cuinchy

XX
2

Auchy

Cambrin

Béthune

Haisnes

Douvrin

GOUGH

XXX
I

Corons
Fosse
8

3 Cabarets

XX

Stützpunkt I

XX
9

Hohenzollern
Redoubt

Quarries

Cité St Elie

Vermelles

Stützpunkt II

XX
7

Bois
Carré

Benifontaine

XXX

Hulluch

La Rutoire

XX
1

Stützpunkt III

Fosse
3

Lone
Tree

Puis 13 bis

Stützpunkt IV

XX
15

XX

Chalk Pit
Wood

Bois Hugo

Stützpunkt V

RAWLINSON

XXX
IV

Loos Road
Redoubt

Puis 14 bis

Fosse
6

Fosse
7

Loos

Chalet
Wood

Lens Road
Redoubt

Cité
St Auguste

XX
47

'Tower
Bridge'

Hill 70
Redoubt

Grenay

North Maroc

Garden
City

Loos Crassier

Fosse
5

Copse

Double Crassier

Cité
St Edouard

Cité
St Laurent

South Maroc

Cité
St Pierre

Lens

N

0   1000 yards

0   1000 m

XX British assaulting divisions, 25 Sept. 1915
- - - British front line before the attack of 25 Sept. 1915
•••••• British line at night on 25–26 Sept. 1915
- - - British line at the end of the battle, 14 Oct. 1915
— — — German front line, 25 Sept. 1915
——— German second line

retain the reserves under GHQ's control until the attack developed, although he did accede to Haig's request that the heads of the two leading divisions of XI Corps should be within four to six miles of the start line on the morning of the assault. The choice of XI Corps for this role was in itself curious, since two of its three divisions had been in France less than a month.

Following a four-day bombardment the gas was released at 5.50 am on 25 September, 40 minutes before the infantry assault. The gas largely failed in the centre and on the left, drifting back over the British trenches in places. Nevertheless, the 9th (Scottish) Division overcame the daunting defences of the Hohenzollern Redoubt and Fosse 8, while the 15th (Scottish) Division captured Loos village. Receiving Haig's request for the reserves at 8.45 am, Sir John French freed the inexperienced 21st and 24th Divisions by 9.30. However, the slow transmission of orders and congestion in the rear – partly the fault of Haig's staff – delayed their arrival. They were forced to march at night, over unknown and debris-strewn terrain, for an attack the next morning, without artillery support, against the uncut wire of the German second position between Lens and Hulluch. It is small wonder that their attack dissolved into a disorganised retirement. The Germans soon recaptured many of the earlier British gains, including the Hohenzollern Redoubt.

The French, anxious not to repeat their mistakes of May, placed *their* own reserves too far forward on this occasion and suffered severe casualties from artillery fire. Even so, their Tenth Army finally seized Souchez on 26 September. The Germans kept possession of Vimy Ridge but the French took an important knoll – later called 'The Pimple' – at its northern end, and held this feature for nearly five months. A further British attack on the Hohenzollern Redoubt on 13 October only secured its western face.

These scattered tactical prizes were trifling rewards for the Allies, the Artois offensive having cost over 50,000 British casualties and approximately 48,000 French. German losses overall totalled about 56,000. In the BEF,

Sir John French can rightly be censured for keeping the reserves too far back and retaining control of them too long. That said, the tactical handling of those reserves by Haig and his staff, once they came under First Army's direct orders, was unimpressive. Clearly the BEF – not least its senior commanders – had much still to learn, although the combat performance of the Scottish New Army divisions – 9th and 15th – offered some encouragement for the future.

Haig takes command of the BEF

Sir John French was swept away by the recriminations over the handling of the reserves at Loos and was succeeded as Commander-in-Chief of the BEF by Douglas Haig on 19 December 1915. Historians disagree about the extent to which Haig manipulated the situation to his own advantage. Increasingly disenchanted with

General Sir Douglas Haig, Commander-in-Chief of the British Expeditionary Force from December 1915. He was promoted to Field-Marshal at the end of 1916. (IWM)

his superior since Mons, Haig had certainly taken care to ensure that his feelings about French were known in the corridors of power. One should note, however, that,

Bombers of the 1st Battalion, Scots Guards, priming Mills grenades in Big Willie Trench, near Loos, October 1915. (IWM)

within a few months Haig's blend of single-minded professionalism and growing pragmatism had helped to generate fundamental improvements in the infrastructure, organisation, equipment and tactics of the BEF. His influence was also apparent in the appointment of Lieutenant-General Sir William Robertson as

Chief of the Imperial General Staff (CIGS) on 23 December. Before accepting that post, Robertson insisted that the CIGS should be the Cabinet's only authoritative source of advice on operations. Though not uncritical of Haig, Robertson broadly supported the latter's opinion that the war would be won in France. The decision to evacuate Gallipoli having already been reached, the elevation of Haig and Robertson virtually guaranteed the primacy of the Western Front in British strategic policy in 1916.

It was now evident to Allied generals that protracted operations were the prerequisite of decisive victory. The battles of 1915 had established that methodical planning, intense bombardments and furious infantry assaults would usually lead to the capture of enemy front positions but the problems of exploiting the 'break-in' seemed intractable. With the German positions becoming stronger and deeper, the Allies had yet to surmount the difficulties of launching a series of attacks on successive positions, with each requiring fresh reserves and artillery preparation. Furthermore, while acknowledging the necessity of attrition, Allied commanders had not relinquished all hopes of a breakthrough and did not entirely appreciate that attrition worked best when the ground seized was not itself of great importance except as bait to lure in and eliminate as many enemy troops as possible. Indeed, many senior Allied commanders remained wedded to the idea of seizing particular objectives rather than conceiving limited offensives to kill the maximum number of Germans.

There had been some new developments in tactics during 1915. By the end of the year the Germans were moving away from the columns and skirmish lines of 1914 and were training special assault detachments, or 'storm troops', which had their own flamethrowers, light artillery and mortars for close fire support and advanced independently to deal with enemy strongpoints. In France, flexible infantry tactics were similarly promoted by Captain André Laffargue, who wrote a seminal

An aerial view of trench lines in the Auchy sector, between Loos and La Bassée, November 1915. (IWM)

pamphlet on *The Attack in Trench Warfare*. The British – struggling to cope with the huge influx of citizen soldiers in the expanding BEF – were currently less progressive in tactical thinking, but the appearance of the Stokes mortar and Mills grenade, as well as a conspicuous rise in munitions production, indicated that they would shortly begin to win the vital war of matériel.

At an inter-Allied conference at Chantilly from 6 to 8 December it was concluded that to counter the Central Powers' ability to shift reserves rapidly from theatre to theatre on interior lines of communication the Allies should launch simultaneous offensives in 1916 on the Italian, Eastern and Western fronts. Joffre proposed to Haig, at the end of December, that the main Franco-British blow might be struck astride the River Somme. On 23 January 1916 he suggested that, prior to the offensive, the BEF should engage the Germans in 'wearing-out fights' in April and May. Haig saw such actions as a key preliminary phase of the main battle, not as separate operations. Determined to avoid squandering the under-trained BEF

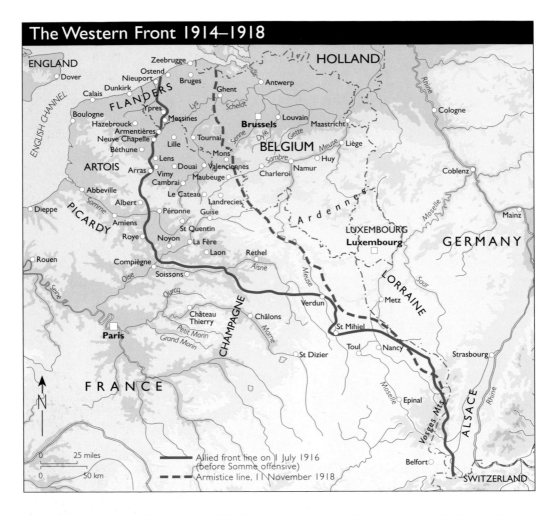

The Western Front 1914–1918

Allied front line on 1 July 1916
(before Somme offensive)

Armistice line, 11 November 1918

prematurely, he resisted this aspect of Joffre's proposals. While personally favouring a Flanders offensive, Haig was nonetheless sharply aware that Britain was still the junior partner in the military alliance. Consequently he agreed with Joffre, on 14 February, that the BEF would play its part in a joint offensive on the Somme around 1 July 1916.

Attrition in the ascendant

Even as the Allies were formulating their plans for 1916, the Germans were preparing to beat them to the punch. There were currently no serious threats to the Central Powers in the east, so Falkenhayn could at last think again about attacking in the west,

where a major victory was clearly required to nullify the growing Allied superiority in men and matériel. Britain, seen by Falkenhayn as the 'arch-enemy', might eventually be brought to heel by unrestricted submarine warfare, but attacks on neutral shipping also risked causing a wrathful United States to join the Allies.

Another solution, on land, might be to convince France that further sacrifice was futile, thereby knocking Britain's 'best sword' from her hand. The events of 1915 had shown that a mass breakthrough was unlikely, so Falkenhayn decided instead to order a limited offensive in a specially selected sector which the French would defend at any cost. In such an action, Falkenhayn reasoned, 'the forces of France will bleed to death' as successive waves of French reinforcements were lured within range of a gigantic concentration of German artillery.

Falkenhayn's chosen killing ground was the fortress-city of Verdun, a symbol of French national pride located in a salient which German guns could bombard from three sides. The offensive would be conducted by the German Fifth Army under Crown Prince Wilhelm, the heir to the throne, thus ensuring the Kaiser's support. (In fact, the real authority in the Fifth Army lay with its Chief of Staff, von Knobelsdorf, the Kaiser's own appointee. 'Whatever he advises you, you must do,' the Kaiser pointedly informed his son.)

Almost encircled by ridges and hills on both banks of the Meuse, Verdun was also protected by rings of forts. The strongest, in theory, was Fort Douaumont, perched on a 1,200-foot height north-east of the city, on the right bank. However, the strength of the forts was illusory, many of their guns having been removed to provide extra firepower for the French autumn operations. A member of the Chamber of Deputies, Emile Driant, had infuriated Joffre by disclosing Verdun's weaknesses to fellow Deputies. By a remarkable twist of fate, Driant, in February 1916, was commanding two battalions of *Chasseurs* in the Bois des Caures – a feature at the epicentre of the German attack.

It is open to debate whether Falkenhayn actually meant to seize Verdun. His decisions to strike the initial blow with only nine divisions, to keep reserves under his own control and to restrict the assault to the right bank all indicate that this was not his principal aim. On the other hand, Crown

Soldiers of the French 68th Infantry Regiment in a dug-out in the Ravin de Souchez, October 1915. (IWM)

Prince Wilhelm was encouraged to proceed with planning on the assumption that the objective was to capture Verdun 'by precipitate methods'. Not for the first time, nor indeed the last, confusion about strategic purpose infected German offensive operations. The immediate task of secretly massing over 1,220 artillery pieces behind the German front was meticulously carried out but nobody could influence the weather. Gales, rain and blizzards forced Falkenhayn to delay the assault – scheduled to start on 12 February – for nine days.

Attack at Verdun

The battle opened at dawn on 21 February. A single 38cm naval gun, 20 miles from the city, fired the first round at a bridge spanning the Meuse. This shell, which missed its target, was the prelude to a nine-hour bombardment of unprecedented savagery. More than 80,000 shells fell in the Bois des Caures alone. With their rearward communications severed, the bewildered defenders were in no condition to repel a major assault. Fortunately for the French, the

German planners had been too cautious, limiting infantry operations on the first day to strong fighting patrols which would employ infiltration tactics to seek out weak spots in the French line. Only the VII Reserve Corps commander, von Zwehl, disregarded these orders and showed what might have been achieved. He deployed storm troops just behind the fighting patrols and, in five hours, secured the Bois d'Haumont. In the Bois des Caures, however, Driant's shrewd use of strongpoints instead of continuous trench lines enabled the

surviving *Chasseurs* to defend that position obstinately against the German XVIII Corps.

On 22 February von Zwehl was again the pace-setter, bursting through a regiment of Territorials on the French 72nd Division's left at the Bois de Consenvoye and then seizing Haumont to tear open a gap in the French first line and expose the left flank of the Bois des Caures. During the late afternoon the heroic Driant was killed whilst endeavouring to withdraw his shattered battalions to Beaumont. Much of the French front line had crumbled but despite terrible casualties the defenders were inflicting increasing losses on the Germans, especially among their key storm troops. The next day the Germans came up against an intermediate line that had only recently been created on De Castelnau's orders and so was not marked on German maps. The dogged defence of Herbebois by the French 51st Division was overcome that evening but overall German gains were disappointing on 23 February. The 37th African Division began to reach the battlefield to shore up the depleted units of the French XXX Corps and, ominously for the Germans, powerful French artillery was massing on the left bank of the Meuse.

In the short term these developments were of scant comfort to the French. Before dawn on 24 February Samogneux was in German hands. The French 51st and 72nd Divisions were close to collapse. Beaumont then fell and in barely three hours the French second position broke apart. Algerian Zouaves and Moroccan *Tirailleurs* of the 37th Division, committed piecemeal to the battle and with no protection from the bitter cold or the fury of the German guns, could not stabilise the situation. Indeed, the 3rd Zouaves – facing the Brandenburgers of the German III Corps – melted away, so uncovering Fort Douaumont, a pivotal point in the defences. As darkness descended, the leading elements of Balfourier's French XX Corps arrived to relieve the battered XXX Corps but there was no guarantee that these fresh troops could repair the disintegrating front.

A German MG08 machine-gun crew in action. (IWM)

Fort Douaumont is captured

On 25 February the 24th Brandenburg
Regiment entered the gap left by the
3rd Zouaves. Some detachments pushed
beyond the stipulated objectives as far as Fort
Douaumont. Here, partly because of a French
staff and command muddle, the garrison
numbered less than 60. Emboldened by the
curious inactivity of the fort, a few pioneers,
under a sergeant named Kunze, pressed
through the outer defences to the dry moat.
Still undetected, they climbed through a gun
embrasure in to one of the fort's galleries.
Though German 42cm shells had not
inflicted critical damage on the fort, the
shock waves and fumes they produced had
driven the defenders to shelter in the bowels
of the fort. Kunze was followed in by three
more small groups of Brandenburgers and the
dejected garrison surrendered by 4.30 pm.

The capture of such a prize at minimal
cost sparked national rejoicing in Germany.
The attackers appeared to have a clear route
into Verdun and the commander of the
French Central Army Group, De Langle de
Cary, had already advocated withdrawal to
the heights to the east and south-east.
However, the combative De Castelnau, at
French General Headquarters, opposed this
policy. Having ensured that Pétain's Second
Army would be brought out of reserve to
hold the left bank of the Meuse, he travelled
to Verdun on 25 February and scotched all
thoughts of retirement. He also called for
Pétain's area of responsibility to embrace the
right bank of the Meuse, which was to be
defended at all costs. To some extent these
measures were playing into Falkenhayn's
hands, yet, as De Castelnau knew, French
doctrine and national sentiment made it
inconceivable to abandon Verdun.

Like Plumer at Ypres in 1915, the
pragmatic Pétain's preference would probably
have been controlled withdrawal. However, as
an unambitious officer who shunned intrigue
and ostentation, Pétain was ideally suited to
the role in which he was now cast. Again like
Plumer, he understood modern firepower and
was trusted by his troops. His very presence at

General (later Marshal) Henri Philippe Pétain who,
as commander of the French Second Army, ably
conducted the defence of Verdun in the spring of 1916.
(Hulton Deutsch)

Verdun lifted morale and he inspired renewed
confidence in the Verdun forts as the
backbone of a 'Line of Resistance'. French
artillery was concentrated to give the
Germans a taste of attrition. Above all, Pétain
grasped the importance of logistics. As rail
links to Verdun were cut by German long-
range artillery, he took pains to ensure that
supplies were maintained along the single
viable route south – a road which became
known as the *Voie Sacrée* (Sacred Way). By
June vehicles were moving up and down this
lifeline at the rate of one every 14 seconds.

Spring and summer fighting at Verdun

The German advance was, in truth, already
losing impetus before Pétain's measures
began to take effect. Falkenhayn had made

few reserves available and Fifth Army now rued its earlier caution in deferring the main infantry attack until the second day. As fire increased from French artillery on the left bank of the Meuse – particularly from guns near the Bois Bourrus ridge and a hill known as *Le Mort Homme* (The Dead Man) – the Germans also regretted confining their first attack to the right bank. Persuaded by the Crown Prince and von Knobelsdorf that this flanking fire must be suppressed, Falkenhayn provided more troops so that the offensive could be extended to the left bank. A major attack, centred on *Le Mort Homme*, would be made on 6 March, followed quickly by a renewed push on the right bank towards Fort Vaux. The Crown Prince, for one, wanted the battle to be terminated once German casualties exceeded French losses.

The sombre pattern of the Verdun fighting for months to come was firmly established in March. All German attempts to seize *Le Mort Homme* failed, and each assault invariably prompted a French counter-attack. Artillery fire from both sides

was unrelenting. By the end of March German casualties totalled 81,607, only 7,000 fewer than the French.

To improve the morale and freshness of French units, Pétain introduced the 'Noria' system, rotating them more frequently in and out of the line, whereas the Germans kept formations at the front for longer periods. The BEF's relief of the French Tenth Army at Arras further ameliorated French manpower difficulties.

The Germans too adjusted their command structure at Verdun, giving General von Gallwitz responsibility for the left bank and entrusting the right bank to General von Mudra, but April passed with *Le Mort Homme* and the neighbouring height, *Côte 304*, still beyond their clutches.

Wavering between ruthlessness and self-doubt, Falkenhayn started to ponder the possible need to 'seek a decision elsewhere',

The commander of the German Fifth Army, Crown Prince Wilhelm, talking to a stretcher-bearer on a visit to the front. (IWM)

A German infantryman shelters in a damaged trench beside the body of a French soldier. (IWM)

and the Crown Prince harboured even greater reservations about prolonging the battle. Knobelsdorf, however, had no such misgivings, and exploited his unique position to gain Falkenhayn's backing for further attacks. He also succeeded in getting the pessimistic von Mudra replaced with the aggressive von Lochow. After a heavier bombardment than that of 21 February the Germans took *Côte 304* early in May and had seized the whole of *Le Mort Homme* by the end of the month, albeit at frightful cost.

Pétain's achievements in slowing the Germans were hardly extolled by Joffre, who wished him to adopt a more offensive stance and was worried that the 'Noria' system was soaking up reserves required for the Somme. Joffre's solution was to elevate Pétain to the command of the Central Army Group and

appoint Robert Nivelle as Pétain's successor at Second Army. Nivelle, a fervent disciple of the Foch–Grandmaison philosophy, took direct control of the battle on 1 May. Another officer who now strode to centre stage was Charles Mangin, a divisional commander nicknamed 'The Butcher' or 'Eater of Men' because of his belief in attacking regardless of losses. Rejecting Pétain's wise advice to wait until he had enough men to strike on a broader front, Mangin – with the approval of Joffre and Nivelle – hurled his 5th Division into a murderous yet vain attempt to recapture Fort Douaumont on 22/23 May.

The battle now created its own momentum, resembling an all-consuming monster impossible to control. Attack-minded commanders on both sides ensured that there would be no pause in the slaughter. Disappointed at the negligible progress on the right bank, Knobelsdorf won Falkenhayn's endorsement for a new five-division assault in

The damaged south-west face of Fort Vaux following the battle of Verdun in 1916. (IWM)

this sector. The attack, codenamed *May Cup*, commenced on 1 June with the objectives of capturing Fort Vaux, Fort Souville and the strongpoint called the *Ouvrage de Thiaumont* – seen as the final obstacle shielding Verdun.

At Fort Vaux the garrison fought valiantly, disputing every yard of the dark underground passages against grenade, gas and flamethrower attacks before extreme thirst forced them to capitulate on 7 June. The next day the Germans took hold of the *Ouvrage de Thiaumont*, only to lose it again almost immediately. In a miniature version of the whole battle, this feature would change hands 14 times between then and 24 October. Pétain's 'Line of Resistance' was cracking, and he was becoming ever more irritated by British inaction on the Somme. Joffre's marshalling of reserves for the Somme offensive, combined with Nivelle's profligacy with troops in incessant counterattacks at Verdun, undermined the benefits of the 'Noria' system. By 12 June the Second Army had just one fresh brigade in reserve.

The Germans, however, were hamstrung by their own manpower problems at the critical moment, since Brusilov's offensive against the Austrians on 4 June had forced Falkenhayn to release three divisions from the west for the Eastern Front. Undeterred, Knobelsdorf brushed aside the Crown Prince's objections to further assaults and assembled sufficient troops, including the splendid Alpine Corps, to attack Fort Souville, less than three miles from Verdun.

By mid-1916 the German Army, like its opponents, was exploring the potential of the 'creeping barrage', which helped infantry advance towards objectives behind a moving curtain of fire. At the same time the Germans were placing greater emphasis on infiltration tactics, whereby specialist assault teams and storm troops were trained to bypass strongpoints and drive deep into enemy positions before striking them from the rear and flanks. When Fort Souville was attacked on 23 June the Germans used 'Green Cross' shells filled with deadly phosgene gas – principally to silence the

The battle of Verdun, February–December 1916

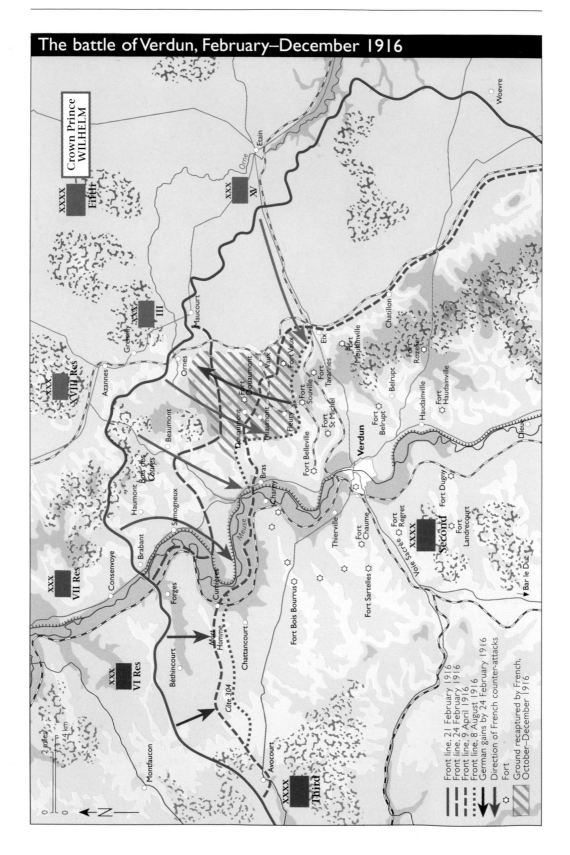

Front line, 21 February 1916
Front line, 24 February 1916
Front line, 9 April 1916
Front line, 8 August 1916
German gains by 24 February 1916
Direction of French counter-attacks
Fort
Ground recaptured by French,
October–December 1916

French gunners – and took Fleury. This success roused Nivelle to issue an Order of the Day which ended with the immortal phrase: *Ils ne passeront pas!* (They shall not pass!). The Germans were indeed halted and contributed to their own failure by attacking on a narrow frontage with inadequate reserves.

While the original aim of the Verdun offensive had long since been obscured, the cost in blood had been too high for either side to risk national dishonour by becoming the first to terminate the battle. The intransigent Knobelsdorf ordered one more assault on Fort Souville on 11 July and some 30 soldiers reached its glacis, within sight of Verdun, before they were pushed back, captured or killed.

This was the nearest the Germans came to Verdun. The opening of the Somme offensive on 1 July changed the whole strategic picture and Falkenhayn directed the Fifth Army to 'adopt a defensive attitude'. The Crown Prince's wishes were finally granted on 23 August, when the Kaiser sanctioned Knobelsdorf's transfer to the Eastern Front. Romania's entry into the war on the Allied side four days later precipitated the downfall of Falkenhayn, who had insisted this would not occur. He was succeeded as Chief of the General Staff by Field Marshal von Hindenburg, who brought with him his own Chief of Staff – Ludendorff, the hero of Liège – whose impact on the Western Front would be immense.

The French counterstroke

Ludendorff, who had helped mastermind most of the German victories in the east, knew how important he was to Hindenburg and demanded the title 'First Quartermaster General' rather than 'Second Chief of the General Staff'. He was also given joint responsibility for all decisions, and from then on Hindenburg's leadership became largely symbolic. Ludendorff assumed almost dictatorial powers, wielding enormous influence over German political affairs, the economy and foreign policy as well as on military operations.

A French 105mm gun being loaded, 1916. (IWM)

After visiting the Western Front in early September Hindenburg and Ludendorff made crucial changes in German tactics and strategy. On 2 September a strict defensive posture at Verdun was decreed. Falkenhayn's rigid linear defence tactics – holding ground at all costs and, when lost, recapturing it by instant counter-attack – was superseded by a flexible zonal defence system, as recommended by the First Army's Chief of Staff, Colonel von Lossberg. This included a thinly held outpost zone in front of the main battle or defence zone and strong counter-attack formations kept close at hand but beyond enemy artillery range. Hindenburg and Ludendorff also ordered the construction of new defensive positions behind the existing lines. These rear positions, embodying the latest principles of elastic defence, were built in great depth but reduced the overall length of front, enabling the Germans to achieve economies in manpower.

To the German soldiers facing the inevitable French counterstroke at Verdun, these changes were of little immediate assistance. With Pétain ensuring that there would be sufficient artillery and infantry to attack on a broad front, the French blow was planned by Nivelle but would be delivered by Mangin, now commanding the French forces on the right bank. More than 650 artillery pieces were assembled, including two 40cm railway guns for use against Fort Douaumont. As one of its leading champions, Nivelle relied heavily upon the creeping barrage, although this time the artillery supporting the infantry concentrated more on suppressing German troops than on destroying particular targets and field fortifications. These tactics would prove highly effective when the initial counterstroke was made on 24 October: the *Ouvrage de Thiaumont* and Fleury were rapidly retaken that day, as was Fort Douaumont, which fell to Moroccan troops. Fort Vaux was recaptured on 2 November, much of the ground lost between February and July was regained, and on 15 December another attack carried the French lines two miles beyond Douaumont. The Germans, however, clung on to *Le Mort Homme*.

This last convulsion brought the agony of Verdun to an end. French casualties tallied

A captured German machine gun being fired by French soldiers at Fort Douaumont, Verdun. (IWM)

377,000 as against 357,000 German. Nobody had secured any discernible advantage from the slaughter. Falkenhayn's irresolution and failure to reconcile the means to the end had caused his original strategy to backfire; in the process he drained the lifeblood from the German Army as well as from the French. Indeed, neither side would completely recover from the battle before the Armistice.

Preparing for the Somme

By June 1916 the BEF comprised well over a million men. Its 48 divisions were organised into five armies and included formations from Australia, Canada, India, New Zealand, Newfoundland and South Africa. This expansion was the product of colossal feats of improvisation in Britain and her Dominions since August 1914. The decline of voluntary recruiting had forced Britain to introduce conscription for single men in January 1916 and married men in May that year. However, compulsory service had not yet made an impact on the BEF, which, alone among the major armies in mid-1916, was still composed

of volunteers. Many of these were in Territorial units or in the divisions of the 'New Armies' recruited in response to Kitchener's appeals. The BEF's highly localised character was typified by its 'Pals' battalions, raised by civilian committees and made up of workmates, friends or men with a common social or geographical background. As the Territorials too were recruited from comparatively narrow geographical areas, in 1916 the BEF embraced many units which had close links with particular communities. Of the 247 infantry battalions that would be in the front line or immediate reserve on the Somme on 1 July, 141 were New Army formations. Though full of confident and enthusiastic volunteers, relatively few of these units had participated in a major battle. However, the New Zealand Division and the four Australian divisions that reached France by June did contain a fair nucleus of men who had seen action at Gallipoli.

The choice of the Somme region in Picardy for the Franco-British offensive in

As Secretary-of-State for War from August 1914 to June 1916, Field-Marshal Lord Kitchener (above) created Britain's first ever mass army. (Ann Ronan Picture Library)

1916 was largely determined by the fact that it marked the junction of the French and British forces. Its drawbacks were that no great strategic objectives, such as rail centres, lay close behind the German front and also that, because the sector had long been quiet, the Germans had constructed formidable defences in the Somme chalk, including dug-outs up to 40 feet below ground. Between February and June the demands of Verdun had reduced the French contribution to the Somme assault to only 11 divisions. For the first time in the war the British would therefore play the leading role in an Allied offensive on the Western Front.

Haig's intention was that, on the first day, Rawlinson's Fourth Army – created on 1 March – should take the German front

defences from Serre to Montauban, then the German second position from Pozières to the Ancre and the slopes in front of Miraumont. The 46th and 56th Divisions, on the northern flank, would attempt to pinch out the German salient at Gommecourt in a diversionary operation. To their right, the 31st, 4th and 29th Divisions (VIII Corps) would attack between Serre and Beaumont Hamel. On the other side of the Ancre, the 36th (Ulster) and 32nd Divisions (X Corps) were to assault the daunting Thiepval defences, including the Schwaben and Leipzig Redoubts. The 8th and 34th Divisions (III Corps) would attack Ovillers and La Boisselle, astride the Albert–Bapaume road; XV Corps, with the 21st, 17th and 7th Divisions, was to secure Fricourt and Mametz; and on Rawlinson's right, next to the French, the 18th and 30th Divisions (XIII Corps) would capture Montauban. North and south of the River Somme itself, General Fayolle's French Sixth Army would assist the British advance by attacking towards the German second position opposite Péronne, between Maurepas and Flaucourt. Should the initial assault gain its objectives, Haig aimed to burst through the German second position on the higher ground between Pozières and Ginchy and, in due course, capture the enemy third position in the Le Sars–Flers sector, thus threatening Bapaume. This might, in turn, clear the way for Hubert Gough's Reserve Army, formed on 23 May, to swing northwards, in the direction of Arras.

British planning for the Somme was muddled by fundamental differences between the operational ideas of Haig and Rawlinson. As at Loos, Haig hoped for a breakthrough; Rawlinson favoured 'bite and hold' tactics, whereby the advancing troops would consolidate gains and shatter German counter-attacks as the artillery was brought forward for the next bound. Rawlinson's object was 'to kill as many Germans as possible with the least loss to ourselves'. As Haig's subordinate, he strove to follow his chief's general directive but because Haig entrusted the detailed planning to

ABOVE Recruits of the Sheffield City Battalion (12th York and Lancaster Regiment) drilling at Bramall Lane football ground, September 1914. (IWM)

BELOW Portrait of Lieutenant-General Sir Henry Rawlinson, commander of the British Fourth Army, on the steps of his headquarters at Querrieu in 19160. (IWM)

Rawlinson – and since their differences in operational approach were neither adequately discussed nor settled – the final scheme for the assault was riddled with contradictions, faulty assumptions and misunderstandings. Rawlinson's tactical guidance to his own subordinates was equally open to different interpretations. His lingering reservations about the ability of New Army divisions to execute complicated manoeuvres were reflected in the *Fourth Army Tactical Notes*, issued in May 1916. Rawlinson observed that his relatively inexperienced citizen-soldiers had 'become accustomed to deliberate action based on precise and detailed orders' and recommended that the assaulting troops 'must push forward at a steady pace in successive lines', though he also stressed 'celerity of movement' and, later in the *Notes*, suggested that small columns making use of natural cover, 'are preferable during the preliminary stages of the advance'. He did not, however, *dictate* the pace at which troops crossed No Man's Land; nor did he insist on particular formations. The ambiguity of his instructions gave corps, divisional and brigade commanders scope to determine their own assault pace and

Riflemen and a Lewis gunner of the 2nd Australian Division in a trench at Croix du Bac, near Armentières, 18 May 1916. (IWM)

formations with the unfortunate result that, in some sectors, over-rigid artillery timetables and infantry tactics were adopted.

This need not have mattered too much had the artillery been able to negate the distinct tactical advantages the Germans enjoyed on the Somme. Unhappily for the Fourth Army, the apparently irresistible week-long preliminary bombardment by 1,537 guns was inadequate to the task. It was widely anticipated that the artillery would destroy the German defences to such an extent that the initial assault would be a 'walk-over' and the pace of the advance therefore immaterial. In reality the number of heavy guns (467) proved too few, they relied too heavily on shrapnel rather than high explosive shells to smash trenches and cut wire, many of the rounds fired were 'duds' and the guns were spread too thinly along the front to produce the desired effect.

The bloody first day

At 7.30 am on 1 July 1916 the British barrage lifted from the enemy front trenches. Along a 14-mile stretch, Rawlinson's infantry moved forward – many in long lines. In most places on that hot morning the attackers lost the 'race to the parapet', failing to get through the enemy's wire and into the front trenches before the Germans came up from their deep dug-outs to man their machine guns. This time Rawlinson had misjudged the difficulties in seizing the German front line in a set-piece assault. Thanks to their dug-outs and the British artillery's inability to destroy the wire, many Germans survived the bombardment to mow down the attackers in rows as the latter tried to cross No Man's Land at a steady pace. To add to the Fourth Army's problems, British counter-battery work was largely ineffective and hitherto unlocated German guns now opened fire, increasing the scale of slaughter.

The explosion of huge mines under the German trenches at La Boisselle, in the British 34th Division's area, and at Hawthorn

Redoubt, on the front of VIII Corps, did not materially assist the attack. In fact, the ill-conceived decision by VIII Corps to lift its barrage when the Hawthorn Redoubt mine was detonated at 7.20 am merely gave the defenders an additional ten minutes to line their parapets and contribute to the British disaster between Serre and Beaumont Hamel. Elsewhere along the British front, over-optimistic and rigid fire plans – with the artillery lifting from one objective to another in accordance with an inflexible timetable – not only carried the barrage too far ahead of the infantry but also meant that it was well-nigh impossible to bring it back.

Even on that bloody morning the story was not one of unrelieved misery. On the southern flank of Fourth Army, where the attackers were much helped by the presence of French heavy guns on their right, the 30th and 18th Divisions, using more imaginative tactics, captured all their objectives in the Carnoy–Montauban sector. Next to them, the 7th Division took Mametz. The percipient Major-General Ivor Maxse, commanding the 18th (Eastern)

The British mine, containing 40,000lbs of ammonal, explodes under the Hawthorn Redoubt at 7.20 am, 1 July 1916. (IWM)

Division, moved his assaulting infantry into No Man's Land before zero hour, giving them a head start in the 'race to the parapet'. He also employed an early form of creeping barrage, as did the 7th Division at Mametz. These limited British successes on 1 July were overshadowed by the progress of Fayolle's French Sixth Army on the right. As well as possessing a preponderance of heavy guns, the French demonstrated that they were digesting the lessons of Verdun, sending their infantry forward in small groups rather than long lines and making better use of available cover.

At other isolated spots on the British front there were tantalising early gains. The battalions of the 36th (Ulster) Division, some of which were also deployed in No Man's Land before the assault, attacked the fearsome defences at Thiepval and, displaying splendid zest and courage, took the Schwaben Redoubt. The comparative lack of

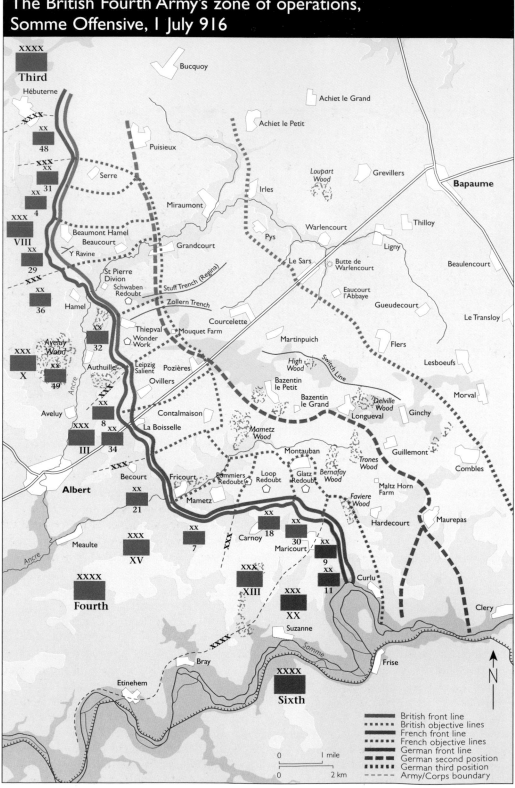

The British Fourth Army's zone of operations, Somme Offensive, 1 July 916

Third XXXX

Hébuterne

Bucquoy

Achiet le Grand

XXXX

XX 48

Achiet le Petit

Puisieux

XXX XX 31

Serre

Loupart Wood

Grevillers

Bapaume

XX 4

XXX

Miraumont

Irles

Warlencourt

Thilloy

Beaumont Hamel

Beaucourt

VIII XX

Y Ravine

Grandcourt

Pys

Le Sars

Ligny

Butte de Warlencourt

Beaulencourt

29

St Pierre Divion

Schwaben Redoubt

Stuff Trench (Regina)

Eaucourt l'Abbaye

Gueudecourt

Le Transloy

XXX XX 36

Hamel

Zollern Trench

Courcelette

Thiepval

Wonder Work

Mouquet Farm

Martinpuich

Flers

Aveluy Wood

XXX

XX 49

Leipzig Salient

Pozières

High Wood

Switch Line

Lesboeufs

X

Authuille

XX 32

Ovillers

Bazentin le Petit

Bazentin le Grand

Delville Wood

Ginchy

Morval

Aveluy

XXX XX

Contalmaison

Longueval

XXX 8 XX 34

La Boisselle

Mametz Wood

Montauban

Guillemont

Combles

III

Becourt

Fricourt

Pommiers Redoubt

Loop Redoubt

Glatz Redoubt

Bernafay Wood

Trones Wood

Maltz Horn Farm

Albert

XX 21

Mametz

Faviere Wood

Hardecourt

Maurepas

Meaulte

XXX **XV**

XX 7

Carnoy

XX 18

Maricourt

XX 30

XX 9

XX

Curlu

Clery

Fourth XXXX

XXX **XIII**

XXX **XX**

XX 11

Suzanne

Somme

Bray

Frise

Etinehem

XXXX **Sixth**

N

	British front line
	British objective lines
	French front line
	French objective lines
	German front line
	German second position
	German third position
	Army/Corps boundary

0   1 mile

0   2 km

The assault of the 103rd (Tyneside Irish) Brigade on La Boisselle, 1 July 1916. (IWM)

movement by neighbouring divisions, however, compelled the Ulstermen to pull back by nightfall. In the north, at Gommecourt, Territorial troops of the 56th (London) Division also captured their objectives but they too were forced to withdraw when the 46th Division was repulsed.

For a shallow penetration – just a mile – on a length of front less than four miles wide the BEF lost 19,240 officers and men killed and 35,493 wounded. The frightful total of 57,470 casualties made 1 July 1916 the bloodiest day ever in British military history. The 34th Division alone – containing four Tyneside Scottish and four Tyneside Irish battalions – incurred 6,380 casualties, and 32 battalions suffered losses of more than 500, or over half their battle strength.

The death or maiming of such a large number of Britain's citizen-soldiers in a single day had a massive effect on the national psyche. Moreover, after the first day of the Somme offensive, the dilution of the highly localised BEF of mid-1916 was inevitable. Partly to lessen the concentrated and dramatic impact of battle losses on particular communities, it became deliberate policy – under a reorganised reserve and drafting system from the summer of 1916 onwards – to draw casualty replacements from a common pool rather than from their parent regiments. In any case, within a few months, conscripts were entering the ranks of the BEF.

Summer on the Somme

For the BEF, 1 July 1916 was undeniably the low point of the entire war. There were many more mistakes, costly setbacks and crises to come, but from that day Haig's forces on the Western Front showed clear signs of a genuine 'learning curve': the subsequent improvements in organisation, command, equipment, tactics and techniques would place the BEF at the cutting edge of the

A wounded man receives treatment in a British trench near Beaumont Hamel, 1 July 1916. (IWM)

Allied armies in 1918. In the high summer of 1916, however, operations on the Somme seemed to offer the front line troops nothing but unending sacrifice. With the slogging match at Verdun already in its fifth month, there could be no question of halting the Somme offensive after only one day. During July Haig began to drop thoughts of a swift breakthrough and to view the Somme fighting more in terms of a 'wearing-out' battle, laying the foundations for a new decisive attack, possibly in mid-September. On the other side, Falkenhayn decreed on 2 July that not one foot of ground should be surrendered, an order which helped initiate the incessant round of British attacks and German counter-attacks that characterised the Somme in 1916.

As July wore on, Gough's Reserve Army took over the northern half of the British zone on the Somme, its junction with Fourth Army running just to the south, or right, of

the Albert–Bapaume road. Haig rejected Joffre's pleas for him to renew the assault in the tricky central sector of his front from Thiepval to Pozières and decided instead to try to exploit the early gains on his right, near Montauban. Accordingly, between 2 and 13 July Rawlinson's Fourth Army tried to take Contalmaison, Mametz Wood and Trones Wood to secure the flanks of a forthcoming attack on the German second main position. Overcoming the reservations of Haig and the French, Rawlinson and the New Army units gave a glimpse of their true capabilities when, on 14 July – after a challenging night assembly in No Man's Land – a 6,000-yard section of the German second position between Bazentin le Petit and Longueval was seized in a few hours. This brilliant feat, which owed much to a more intense artillery bombardment than that before 1 July, had a disappointing sequel. At Delville Wood, near Longueval, the South African Brigade of the 9th (Scottish) Division lost over 2,300 of its 3,153 officers and men in a bitter struggle that lasted from 14 to 21 July. The wood was not completely in British hands until 27 August, while neighbouring High Wood, seemingly empty of German troops on the morning of 14 July, finally fell to Rawlinson two months later, on 15 September.

The Reserve Army, meanwhile, strove to capture the village of Pozières, which, from its dominating position on the Albert–Bapaume road, provided an alternative line of approach into the rear of the Thiepval defences. The Australian divisions of I Anzac Corps underlined their excellent fighting reputation by capturing both the village and the fortified ruins of the windmill on the crest of the ridge beyond by 5 August, but subsequent efforts to move north-west from a constricted salient in the direction of Mouquet Farm and Thiepval were subjected to concentrated German artillery fire. Having suffered some 23,000 casualties in five weeks, the Australians were unsurprisingly critical of Gough's penchant for narrow-front attacks, while a calamitous subsidiary operation at Fromelles on 19/20 July – in which the 5th Australian Division was involved – further diminished Australian confidence in the British High Command. To the south, Rawlinson did his best to assist the French Sixth Army as it crept towards Péronne, but the Fourth Army was unable to capture Guillemont and Ginchy until 3 and 9 September respectively, and Rawlinson was left in no doubt about Haig's dissatisfaction with repeated attacks by inadequate forces on narrow frontages.

Command errors, mounting losses and relentless demands on front line troops were also to be found on the German side of the wire. Falkenhayn's order that from 11 July a strict defensive posture should be maintained at Verdun was a sure indication that British operations on the Somme were having some effect. His insistence on a tactical system of unyielding linear defence and immediate counter-attack – a policy backed by General Fritz von Below of the German Second Army – only added to the strain felt by German divisions. Given less time for rest, reorganisation and training between actions, the strength and quality of German formations began a slow but inexorable decline. The morale of German reinforcements arriving on the Somme correspondingly slumped in the face of the growing Allied superiority in matériel.

Enter the tank

The weeks between mid-July and mid-September brought a change in tactical conditions on the Somme, from siege-type operations to semi-open warfare, in which the Germans often occupied irregular lines of loosely connected shell-holes rather than continuous trenches. After Hindenburg and Ludendorff had replaced Falkenhayn in late August, there was a further shift towards elastic defence in depth, with the German forward positions even more thinly manned.

The British were now using the creeping barrage with greater frequency but it was also becoming imperative for the British and Dominion infantry to vary their tactics, placing less emphasis upon linear 'waves' and more upon the employment of small groups of men who could work their way forward with their own close-support weapons – much in the manner of the assault detachments and storm troops favoured increasingly by the Germans. British infantry platoons and companies needed additional integrated firepower to make them more self-reliant and able to infiltrate between strongpoints instead of invariably carrying out frontal assaults. British gunners likewise continued to place too much faith in prolonged heavy bombardments and centrally controlled fire programmes which were, in fact, inappropriate in attacks on dispersed or thinly-held enemy positions. These developments, and the nature of Haig's 'wearing-out' battle, were not instantly understood by all British divisional commanders and staffs as they strained to prepare more 'line-straightening' actions designed to secure improved jumping-off positions for the next big set-piece assault on a major German defensive system.

Haig faced growing criticism from politicians at home who felt that the limited progress made to date did not justify the dreadful casualties being suffered. The pressure on him to achieve more substantial results from his projected offensive in mid-September was therefore all the greater. Ready to believe the advice of his Chief of Intelligence, Brigadier-General Charteris, that the Germans were approaching exhaustion, Haig was optimistic that a breakthrough might now be forthcoming, especially as his planned large-scale set-piece attack to make on the German third main position would be bolstered by a new weapon, the tank, which had been conceived by Lieutenant-Colonel Ernest Swinton in 1914 as an armoured, tracked vehicle capable of crossing trenches and barbed wire and of destroying enemy machine guns. Swinton had warned against employing tanks in 'driblets' but Haig was keen to use them to deal with separate strongpoints and fortified villages that might otherwise hold up the advancing infantry. He and Rawlinson consequently deployed them along the battle line rather than sending them in to action in one concentrated body.

Haig hoped and anticipated that the breakthrough would be effected by fresh infantry divisions and by the artillery, the density of guns being double that of 1 July though less than half that used for 14 July. As the commander of Fourth Army, which had the principal role, Rawlinson had proposed attacking in stages on three successive nights. He was overruled by Haig, who wanted a bolder attack with no pauses and after Fourth Army's failures in August, Rawlinson was in a weak position to argue his case.

The attack, which began on 15 September, was designed to capture the German third system at Flers, followed by Morval, Lesboeufs and Gueudecourt. The Canadian Corps, part of the Reserve Army to Rawlinson's left, was ordered to seize Courcelette. Forty-nine tanks were assigned to support the infantry on the morning of the attack but only 36 arrived at their starting points. Assisted by a creeping barrage, they caused some alarm and losses

British gunners fire an 18-pounder in the summer heat, near Montauban, 30 July 1916. (IWM)

among the German defenders and in the British 41st Division's sector, four tanks reached Flers. One of these advanced up the main street of the village while the others engaged machine-gun nests and strongpoints on the western and eastern outskirts. Horne's XV Corps took Flers and the Canadian Corps

captured Courcelette, while Martinpuich and High Wood were also secured. Overall, however, on 15 September the gains were restricted to some 2,500 yards on a front of less than three miles. Lesboeufs and Morval held out for a further ten days and Combles and Gueudecourt did not fall until 26 September. Yet again the British offensive became bogged down and the oft-promised breakthrough appeared as far away as ever.

The reckoning

Haig has frequently been censured by historians and military commentators for using tanks prematurely at Flers–Courcelette on 15 September and for deploying them in 'penny packets' rather than in mass formation. Both charges are unfair. Had its debut been postponed, there was no guarantee that this untried weapon would

Infantry advancing in waves in support of the British
XIV Corps attack at Morval, 25 September 1916. (IWM)

then have proved more successful. The Mark I
tanks of 1916 were slow and unreliable and it
might have been an even more serious
blunder to commit them on a large scale
before their merits and shortcomings had
been fully exposed under battle conditions. It
is also often forgotten that Britain was
fighting as part of a coalition: that same day
Allied offensives were proceeding in
Transylvania and on the Italian Front as well
as in the French zone of operations on the
Somme to the south of the BEF. Haig might
therefore be forgiven for reasoning that,
should all go well, a second opportunity to
employ tanks might not actually arise.
Contrary to popular belief, he was certainly
no reactionary so far as weapons technology
was concerned. His enthusiasm for new ideas,
and his personal intervention at critical
moments, encouraged the development and
successful tactical application of Lewis guns,
Mills bombs, trench mortars, gas and aircraft
as well as that of tanks.

Criticism of Haig for prolonging the
British offensive on the Somme after
mid-September is perhaps more justified. His
persistence seems to have been motivated by
the firm belief that the German Army would
indeed eventually collapse provided that the
BEF and its allies did not relax their constant
pressure.

In the last week of September – while the
Fourth Army was attacking towards Morval,
Lesboeufs, Gueudecourt and Combles –
Gough's Reserve Army undertook its biggest
operation so far, assaulting the German
positions from Courcelette to the Schwaben
Redoubt. Mouquet Farm was captured by
the British 11th Division on the opening
day of Gough's attack, 26 September. The
thorough battle training and briefing
given by Ivor Maxse to his 18th Division
paid off, as it cleared Thiepval village early
on 27 September. However, it took until
13 October before the 39th Division was able
to eject the last stubborn defenders from the
Schwaben Redoubt.

On the right flank of the Reserve Army the
Canadian Corps became embroiled in a

A British Mark I tank crosses a trench during the fighting for Thipeval, late September 1916. (IWM)

furious fight for Regina Trench which dragged on until 10 November. On the Fourth Army's front, as rain turned the battlefield into a muddy swamp, Rawlinson's divisions inched painfully towards Le Transloy and secured Le Sars on 7 October.

The last phase of the Somme offensive was carried out by Gough's Fifth Army – as the Reserve Army was renamed – between 13 and 24 November. In spite of several postponements and appalling conditions, the operation was allowed to go ahead in the hope that a late success would create a favourable impression at the inter-Allied conference at Chantilly, which Haig was to attend on 15/16 November. It was hoped also that the attack would have benefits for the Russian and Romanian fronts by dissuading the Germans from switching reserves from France

The Fifth Army's assault on 13 November was delivered astride the River Ancre, north of Thiepval, and was intended to reduce or eliminate the German-held salient between Serre and the Albert–Bapaume road. Employing a creeping barrage, and an overhead heavy machine-gun barrage by Vickers guns, the 51st (Highland) Division captured Beaumont Hamel, and the 63rd (Royal Naval) Division seized Beaucourt. However, Serre – which had been an objective on 1 July – was still occupied by the Germans when Haig brought the offensive to an end. The BEF remained some three miles from Bapaume; all its exertions and sacrifices during the previous four-and-a-half months had resulted in territorial gains measuring about 20 miles wide and six miles deep.

The British and Dominion forces on the Somme suffered a terrifying total of 419,654 casualties. The French, though still short of Péronne, had gained over twice as much ground as the BEF for 204,253 losses – about half the cost. Estimates of German casualties vary hugely – between 237,000 and 680,000. However, statistics alone do not tell the whole story. There was increasing evidence of more progressive tactical thinking in the BEF, with outstanding division and brigade commanders

The battle of the Somme, July–November 1916

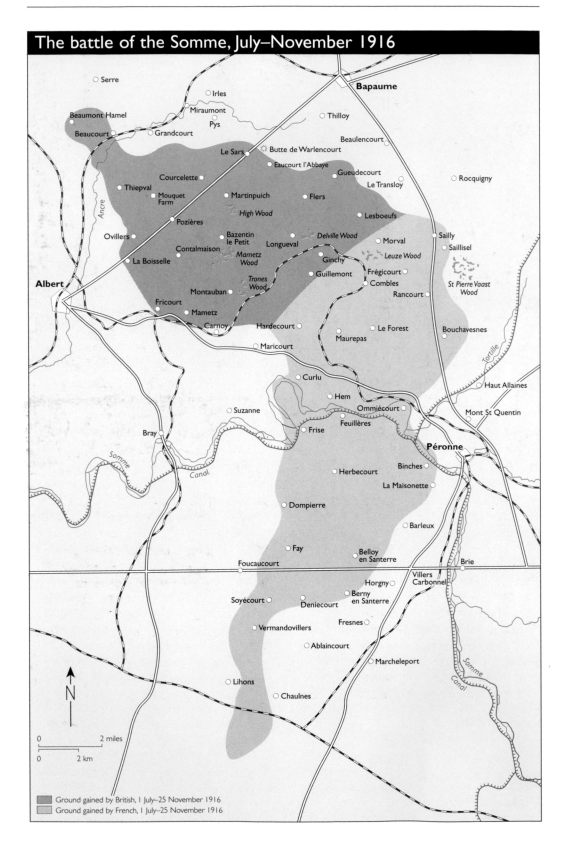

Ground gained by British, 1 July–25 November 1916
Ground gained by French, 1 July–25 November 1916

A British working party, wearing trench waders and waterproof capes, near the Ancre, November 1916. (IWM)

like Maxse of the 18th Division and Solly-Flood of the 35th Brigade urging the adoption of flexible assault formations, meticulous battle training and greater use of Lewis guns and rifle grenades to boost the infantry's own firepower in the attack. The appointment – with Haig's active support – of a civilian expert, Sir Eric Geddes, as Director-General of Transportation at GHQ in September set in train a reorganisation of the BEF's logistics that would eventually pay rich dividends.

The German Army knew that it had been hurt by the improving BEF. On 21 September a Hindenburg memorandum stated that the Somme front was all-important and would have first claim on available divisions. Ludendorff himself admitted that the Army 'had been fought to a standstill and was utterly worn out' and Crown Prince Rupprecht – who faced the BEF for most of the war – observed that what remained of the 'old first-class, peace-trained German infantry had been expended on the battlefield'.

Private Archie Surfleet

Private Archie Surfleet. (IWM)

Although, in the minds of the British public, the story of the first day of the Somme offensive has become particularly associated with the ordeal and sacrifice of the locally raised 'Pals' battalions, not all men in those units on 1 July 1916 were original 1914 recruits. Private Arthur 'Archie' Surfleet, for example, was at Serre that day with the 13th Battalion, East Yorkshire Regiment – one of four battalions raised by the city of Hull – but he had not enlisted until January 1916 and had only joined 'B' Company of his unit at the front on 8 June. From the start, however, he kept a diary, adding details in the 1920s and 1960s to form a lively and lucid account of a young soldier's service.

Archie Surfleet was born at Gainsborough, Lincolnshire, on 23 December 1896 and

moved to Hull with his family in 1901. Educated at Hull Grammar School, he worked as a junior reporter for the *Hull Daily Mail* for about a year before joining a firm of manufacturing chemists, Lofthouse and Saltmer, where his father was a laboratory manager. He enlisted in the Army shortly after his nineteenth birthday. Archie himself confessed to being ' a very ordinary soldier, alternately cheerful and frightened some of the time ... and very frightened indeed for much of it', though he also noted how quickly he and his comrades adjusted to their new life. 'After a period of blissful ignorance', he recalled, 'many of us who saw the front line frequently often acquired a sort of fatalistic outlook, but, by some gift of Providence, we nearly always seemed to remember the happier times and forget much of the horror.'

Archie rapidly became familiar with many of the routine hardships of an infantryman's existence. He described the ubiquitous body lice as one of the most unpleasant things he had to endure – 'as soon as you warmed up they did so too, biting and irritating so that only utter exhaustion could induce sleep'. Rats were also a common nuisance, although 'strangely enough, we got partially used to them'. Some of the more primitive latrines, Surfleet remarked, 'made you feel you had plumbed the depths of indelicacy ... But we even got used to that!' Food was adequate, if never over-plentiful – 'we often popped the rice pud ... unsweetened anyway ... into the bully-stew to give it a bit of "body"'. If one was lucky enough to obtain a quarter of a loaf, 'you felt well-fed and happy', he remembered. The constant demands for working or carrying parties always provoked widespread 'grousing' among the infantry. Even before the Somme offensive, such tasks caused Surfleet to comment that 'we all are as fed [up] as hell with this lot ... The jobs we get are simply heart-breakingly ... almost inhumanly impossible but they have to be done, somehow, and I marvel, daily, that we stick it.'

Entering the battle-zone for a tour of front line duty was always a sobering moment. Approaching the Serre sector for the first time, on 11 June 1916, Surfleet noted 'a kind of torpor peculiar to that shell-infested area came over us'. His introduction to German shelling was 'a terrible experience ... The feeling was so utterly indescribable that I cannot hope to portray it; God alone knows how awfully afraid I was.' Archie estimated that 'not one in a thousand goes "up there" without some qualm or other, though most of the lads seem to be able to disguise their feelings pretty well'. There was one man, however, who suffered from shell-shock at Serre in June and succumbed again in the Laventie sector later in July. He was taken out of the line, Archie recorded, 'a really pitiable sight and most unnerving'.

Once out of the line, morale was swiftly restored. In the autumn of 1916 Archie wrote that the boys 'seem very cheerful just now; a few days of peace and sunshine makes all the difference'. The opportunity to spend some francs from their pay on egg and chips or wine and beer in local *estaminets* helped men briefly forget the terrors of the trenches. Hitherto a strict teetotaller, Surfleet warily sampled his first-ever beer on 6 July: 'I must say I did not find it unpleasant and, so far, I have not felt any of the "after-effects" usually attributed to this stuff!' He did not condemn those who over-indulged in order to blot out the realities of the war. 'There is no wonder those who have a tendency towards drink try to drown their sorrows whenever they get a chance', he commented on 21 July.

Normal grousing aside, Surfleet was clearly a dutiful soldier who respected most of his officers. Theirs was 'a thankless job', he stated in the summer of 1916, later adding, 'I wouldn't be an infantry officer for a mint of money'. He observed with approval how his officers were 'jolly decent' in carrying the rifles of exhausted men during a march in July. He was even impressed by his corps commander, Hunter-Weston, who, in Surfleet's view, 'looked such a real soldier', but he was roused to anger by the sight of a gunner, lashed to a wheel, undergoing Field Punishment No.1. To Surfleet, this seemed 'anti-British' and he wrote that 'feelings amongst our boys' were 'very near to mutiny at such inhuman punishment'.

Archie was fortunate that on 1 July the 31st Division's catastrophic assault on Serre was called off before the Hull battalions, in support, were committed to the attack. In August he was made a linesman with the signallers attached to Battalion Headquarters. Repairing damaged telephone cables under fire was a dangerous job though 'better than the rifleman's life' in Archie's opinion. When his division returned to the Somme for another attack on Serre on 13 November, he was again lucky, being among the troops left in the rear to form the nucleus of a reconstituted battalion in the event of heavy losses. He was, however, required to act as a stretcher-bearer – a harrowing job, but one allowing him to 'look the rest of the lads in the face and claim to be one of them'. Sometimes Archie understandably felt despondent, writing in September, 'our only hope is a good, serious wound to put us out of this lot', yet when in December sickness gave him the opportunity to go to hospital, he declined, not wishing to be parted from his mates. 'This may be hell,' he declared, 'but I'd sooner be here, with my pals, than landed with strangers in another, maybe worse, hell'. Such comradeship was perhaps the biggest single factor in enabling soldiers to bear the horrors of the Western Front.

Surfleet continued to serve as a private until March 1918, when he went home to train for a flying commission in the Royal Flying Corps – soon to become the Royal Air Force. After the war he returned to his previous employers, Lofthouse and Saltmer, and was joint managing director of the firm before retiring in 1962. He died, aged 74, in April 1971, just after depositing a copy of his diary in the Imperial War Museum.

The Home Fronts 1914–1916

The effects of the struggle on the Western Front were felt far beyond the battlefields and had a huge impact on domestic life. Each of the belligerents faced their own special problems. For Britain – dependent upon imports – German submarine operations represented a growing menace; Germany was increasingly affected by the Allied naval blockade; and France had to cope with the early loss of the iron and coal of her German-held northern regions. Certain problems were common to all. Each had to make mammoth efforts to mobilise both human and industrial resources and take unprecedented steps to control raw materials, food production and distribution, prices and wages, the press and transport. In many respects, the manner in which each country responded to these challenges reflected their different political, social and economic conditions.

France

French industry, still over-reliant on small workshops, lagged behind that of Britain and Germany (her steel production in 1914 being less than one-third of German output) but as a predominantly agricultural nation she was largely self-sufficient in food. The declaration of a state of siege in August 1914 allowed the French government to assume almost unlimited powers, subjecting the press, for example, to military censorship. Such measures were vital if René Viviani's administration was to succeed in balancing France's military and industrial priorities.

Conscription in France meant that hardly a single household was left untouched from the outset. By mid-1915 the level of French sacrifice remained much greater than that of Britain, some 5,440,000 having been called

up. With most rural villages denuded of young men, French women were soon bearing a bigger share of agricultural work than ever before, yet many were attracted by the higher wages on offer in the burgeoning munitions factories. Besides those replacing men in public service and commercial jobs, around 75,000 women were working in French munitions plants by October 1915, gaining a previously unknown degree of personal and financial independence.

Swelling criticism of the conduct of the war saw Viviani's government replaced in October 1915 by a broad-based coalition under the Socialist Aristide Briand. In 1916, the year of Verdun, the conflict bit really hard and deep in France, increasing the incipient war-weariness of the civilian population. Lack of price controls meant food costs had soared, and higher wages and the booming profits of war contractors had generated a 40 per cent rise in the cost of living, but despite the destruction of sugar beet factories in northern France, no critical food shortages had so far been suffered. Now, however, difficulties began to surface. To reduce the costs of importing wheat, a coarser 'national bread' was introduced in May 1916; the wheat, rye and potato harvests that year were well below normal; and, in November, a number of restrictions – including meatless days – were agreed in principle, though not all immediately implemented.

Germany

As in France, political parties in Germany concluded a *Burgfrieden* (truce), on 4 August 1914, presenting an image of solid national unity. Germany's autocratic régime could make more rapid decisions than the slower-moving democratic institutions of the

Allies and so could marshal the civilian population more rigorously at an early stage than could Britain and France. More advanced and progressive industrially – particularly in the chemical, electrical, steel and munitions fields – Germany swiftly consolidated these advantages by forming, under the able young businessman Dr Walther Rathenau, a Raw Materials Section of the War Ministry. Through a series of War Raw Materials Corporations, supplies were strictly controlled in different sectors to overcome shortages and, for a time, offset the effects of the Allied blockade.

Germany's quicker transition into top gear was also characterised by her more adroit mobilisation of women. Dr Gertrude Baumer, a leading campaigner for women's rights, was instantly recruited to organise German female labour for war work. Even so, although Germany possessed larger human resources than France, manpower problems were becoming so serious by the end of 1916, after Verdun and the Somme, that more stringent measures were required to augment the labour force. The new High Command team – Hindenburg and Ludendorff – reversed earlier policies in an attempt to secure extraordinary increases in production. Under the so-called Hindenburg Programme, they first created a Supreme War Office for control of the economy and then, on 5 December, pushed through an Auxiliary Service Law providing for the compulsory employment of all German males between 17 and 60 not already in the forces.

It was in food supplies that Germany was most vulnerable. The blockade ensured that this problem would worsen steadily the longer the war continued. Whereas France by mid-1916 had only had to tighten her belt, Germany was approaching a desperate state of shortage. Bread rationing had been introduced as early as January 1915, and potato and meat supplies were also firmly regulated so that, for a while, rising prices rather than scarcities constituted the main worry. In June 1915 the Imperial Grain Office was created to oversee the purchase and distribution of grain; this was the

precursor of similar bodies for other food commodities, culminating in a War Food Office in May 1916. By then meat, potatoes, milk, sugar and butter were all rationed, but partly because of falling imports through neutral countries and also through poor harvests, these measures did not ease the situation. Many elements of diet and even articles of clothing were supplemented or replaced by *Ersatz* or substitute items. A sharp drop in the potato yield, for instance, compelled the German people to switch increasingly to turnips, which became a staple food in the 'turnip winter' of 1916/17.

Britain

For the British – beset before the war by industrial unrest, the militant campaign for women's suffrage and the threat of civil strife over Irish Home Rule – the outbreak of the European conflict also brought a temporary suspension of political discord, although the attempts of Herbert Asquith's Liberal government to carry on along 'business as usual' lines soon foundered. Once the decision to create a mass army had been taken, increased State control of industry and manpower was sure to follow. Paradoxically, an otherwise instinctively anti-interventionist government quickly armed itself with considerable powers with the passage, on 8 August 1914, of the Defence of the Realm Act – DORA. As the war went on, DORA encroached into almost every aspect of daily life and led to the abrogation of personal liberties on a scale inconceivable before August 1914.

The principal need was for more efficient mobilisation and direction of military and industrial manpower. Unrestricted recruiting in the early months and the absence of a rational overall plan meant that problems were tackled in an ad hoc fashion until May 1915, when Britain faced simultaneous crises in enlistment and munitions production. The formation of a coalition Cabinet and the creation of a Ministry of Munitions late that month, however, heralded the end of the government's

"FALL IN, AND FOLLOW ME !"

One of many patriotic postcards published in Britain
during the voluntary recruitment period, 1914–1915.
(Author's collection)

haphazard approach to these issues, although it
was not until 1916 that a more streamlined
War Cabinet was created.

Between August 1914 and December 1915
a total of 2,466,719 men enlisted in the arm,
but by the spring of 1915 it was already
evident that voluntary recruiting would not
suffice to maintain Britain's expanding New
Armies in the field in a long war. From a
peak of 462,901, in September 1914,
enlistments had declined to 119,087 in
April 1915. As calls for conscription
intensified, the government began a more
systematic analysis of its resources by passing
the National Registration Act in July 1915,
empowering the Local Government Board to
compile a register of all persons between
15 and 65. When taken in August, the
National Register revealed that over
5,000,000 men of military age – including
2,179,231 single men – were *not* in the
forces. In the autumn a last effort to uphold
the voluntary principle was undertaken
through a scheme prepared by Lord Derby,
then Director-General of Recruiting. All
males between 18 and 45 were asked to

enlist at once or attest their willingness to
serve when summoned. By the close of the
Derby Scheme, on 30 November, nearly half
the eligible single men on the National
Register had still not attested, making
conscription inevitable in 1916. It was,
however, applied with a velvet glove. From
1 March 1916 to 31 March 1917 only
371,000 men were compulsorily enlisted;
779,936 were granted exemption.

The Munitions of War Act of July 1915
enabled the government to adopt any
measures deemed necessary to expand
production and helped pave the way for
Britain to become a nation in arms. Many
inefficient and wasteful methods were cast
aside and, with trade unions generally ready,
for the time being, to forego some accepted
practices and privileges, the number of strikes
and disputes decreased. Here again women
would play a key part in the process of
industrial mobilisation, performing scores of
tasks hitherto the province of men. Until
mid-1915 much of this effort was channelled
into charity and welfare work. In July 1914
around 212,000 women were employed in the
various metal and engineering industries that
would become most closely linked with war
production; a year later this figure had risen
only to 256,000. With the coming of Lloyd

George's Ministry of Munitions, the figure climbed steeply to 520,000 by July 1916.

The fall in unemployment and higher wages which accompanied government contracts were, as elsewhere, counter-balanced by higher prices – averaging 75 per cent in essential commodities by November 1916. Britain had not yet suffered real shortages, though during 1916 the activities of German submarines caused mounting anxiety in a nation that imported most of its food supplies from overseas. In November 1916 shrinking wheat stocks led to the appearance of 'war bread' and in December the potential seriousness of the situation was signalled with the establishment of a Ministry of Food and the appointment of a Food Controller.

The realities of war had been directly felt by British citizens long before then. Raids on London by German airships had begun at the end of May 1915 and continued through that year and 1916, causing an increase in civilian casualties as well as alarm and disruption. The bombardment of Hartlepool, Scarborough and Whitby by German warships on 16 December 1914 resulted in over 700 casualties, including women and children. A serious *internal* threat also arose on Easter Monday (24 April) in 1916, when Irish nationalists seized the General Post Office in Dublin and proclaimed an Irish Republic. The Easter Rising was suppressed within five days but 64 of the insurgents, around 130 members of the Crown forces and well over 200 civilians were killed. The Rising was, in fact, initially unpopular in Ireland, but the execution in May of 14 of its leaders aroused widespread and lasting public sympathy where little previously existed.

Winnifred Adair Roberts

For many British middle-class women the war presented unexpected outlets for energies and talents that had hitherto remained wholly or partly concealed beneath a veneer of social convention. One such woman was Winnifred Adair Roberts, the seventh of nine children of Frederick Adair Roberts, an Irish-born manufacturing chemist, and his wife Janie. Winnifred, known to her family and friends as Winks, was born on 28 November 1885 in Stamford Hill, London, and in 1900 moved with her parents to Oak Hill Lodge in Hampstead. Educated initially by a governess and later at various establishments, including a Quaker school at Darlington, in the north

of England, she did not pursue a career because delicate health had obliged her to become the 'daughter at home'. A Christian and a spiritualist, she taught at a local Sunday School, though her more independent qualities were revealed by her work for the Women's Social and Political Union. (Her commitment to the cause of women's suffrage was demonstrated by her smuggling of food to the WSPU's leader, Mrs Pankhurst, when the latter was in hiding from the police.)

On holiday in Switzerland at the outbreak of war, Winnifred showed something of her organisational skills by arranging sumptuous provisions for the long train journey across France. Once home, she soon joined the Women's Volunteer Reserve, founded by another eminent suffragette, Evelina Haverfield. The Women's Volunteer Reserve adopted khaki uniforms and military ranks and Winnifred was appointed Captain in command of 'A' Company of the London Battalion.

Besides undertaking canteen duties, hospital work and fund-raising activities, the Company drilled regularly at a skating rink and in the examination hall of the School of Mines in South Kensington, even receiving instruction in rifle-shooting. By August there were 98 members but the average attendance had dropped from 61 to 31 since June. There was some unrest in the Company in June 1915, following work at the Bethnal Green Military Hospital, and Winnifred – who saw the organisation's continuing emphasis on route marches as pointless and came into conflict with her senior officer – resigned on 19 October 1915. However, a stream of sympathetic letters quickly underlined the

Captain Winnifred Adair Roberts (seated centre) with members of 'A' Company of the London Battalion, Women's Volunteer Reserve, 1915. (IWM)

affection and respect in which she was personally held. A week later, 37 former members of 'A' Company met at Winnifred's home and formed a new corps under her command. Within another few days Captain Roberts' Company was attached to the Women's Legion, launched by the Marchioness of Londonderry in July 1915. Convinced that the Women's Volunteer Reserve was drawn from too narrow a class, Lady Londonderry created the Women's Legion to 'provide a capable and efficient body of women whose services can be offered to the State as may be required to take the place of men needed in the firing line or in other capacities'.

Over the next 16 months Winnifred and her colleagues performed a wide range of valuable tasks. These included: eight-hour shifts day or night in canteens and YMCA huts at Euston and King's Cross stations, Woolwich Arsenal, Tottenham Court Road, Holborn and a munitions plant at Erith; bandage-making for the Red Cross; knitting woollen garments and socks; hospital work; and producing sandbags. At Christmas in 1915 Winnifred, with six helpers, catered for some 4,000 soldiers at the canteen in Horseferry Road over a ten-day period, during which the women took just two hours off each night and slept on a table in the basement. Perhaps their biggest achievement, however, was to raise over £445 for a YMCA hut – the 'Captain Roberts Company Hut' – erected near Etaples in France towards the end of 1916. To collect the necessary funds, Winnifred organised jumble sales, bazaars, whist drives, dances, snow-sweeping, carol singing, a garden party and a concert featuring the popular young composer Ivor Novello. Some evenings the women played a barrel-organ, complete with a monkey, in the London streets.

Since many in the group also held other jobs, the strain of such activities eventually began to affect their health. This prompted Winnifred to disband the company in February 1917. She declined to join the new Women's Army Auxiliary Corps (WAAC), which was to be run from the War Office, not only because of her health but also because she felt she was 'already nine-tenths pacifist' and was reluctant to belong to an organisation 'where I am only a "Yes-man". I must be conscience-free and other people's standards are not always my own.' All the same, she later recalled that she had been personally consulted about the uniform, drill and discipline of the Women's Army Auxiliary Corps, that seven of the women she had trained subsequently instructed WAAC recruits and that it was *her* 'girls' who got the responsible positions when the first WAACs went to France. She had good reason to be proud, for in two years Winnifred had made her own distinct contribution to the national war effort.

Despite her fragile health, Winnifred lived to a ripe old age. Developing her interest in spiritualism and the Church, she performed more welfare work in the Second World War, particularly on behalf of the tube shelterers in London during the Blitz. She died in June 1981, aged 95.

No end in sight

As the conflict entered its third year, the almost universal enthusiasm of 1914 had given way to a deepening sense of war-weariness and muted resignation in the belligerent countries. No one could now foresee an early end to this dour, merciless struggle. There was also a growing gulf between front line troops and civilians. Fighting soldiers had undergone experiences that could never be fully understood by those at home. Men snatching a few precious days of leave felt like strangers in their own land and were often dismayed and disturbed by the discrepancies between their own miserly pay and the high wages of war workers; by the soaring profits of war contractors; by the over-optimistic and inaccurate reports in jingoistic newspapers; and by the increasing independence and changed attitudes of wives who were suddenly more prosperous from their employment in munitions factories. For many soldiers, who were becoming closer to their comrades than their families, the trenches were the real world.

Anti-war sentiment in Britain, France and Germany was nowhere strong enough to shake each nation's overall resolve to continue the struggle until outright victory, or at least a favourable peace, had been achieved. Too much blood had been shed for either the Allies or the Central Powers to accept anything less. Tentative peace feelers from both sides in late 1916 came to nothing. Members of the ruling military, conservative and industrial élite in Germany were reluctant to relinquish their annexationist war aims – which included buffer regions to the east and west, and a dependent Belgium – yet were equally unwilling to declare them in precise terms. This presented the Allies, whose governments were also disinclined to be the first to define their intentions, with the excuse to dismiss German peace suggestions as insubstantial and insincere.

In fact, changes of political and military leadership in Britain, France and Germany in the second half of 1916 only intensified each country's pursuit of decisive victory. On 7 December Asquith was succeeded as British Prime Minister by David Lloyd George, who was determined to streamline the machinery of government and prosecute the war with greater vigour. While acknowledging the paramount need for Germany to be defeated, Lloyd George was anxious to discover a strategic alternative to the costly attrition of the Western Front and explore the possibilities offered by other theatres of operations. This policy would bring him into increasing conflict with Haig and Robertson, who wanted to concentrate resources in France.

On 12 December, the dynamic Nivelle replaced the discredited Joffre as French Commander-in-Chief. In Germany, Hindenburg and Ludendorff, who already wielded immense power and influence, similarly stood for total commitment to eventual victory. Indeed, the views of Hindenburg and Ludendorff were much less susceptible to objective military considerations than those of Falkenhayn had been. The latter had paid *some* heed to the limitations of Germany's human and economic resources. In contrast, as the American historian Gerald Feldman has remarked, the new German High Command attempted to implement 'an ill-conceived total mobilisation for the attainment of irrational goals'. In so doing they 'undermined the strength of the army, promoted economic instability, created administrative chaos, and set loose an orgy of interest politics'. With such men at the helm, compromise in 1917 was, at best, unlikely.

Further reading

Asprey, R., *The German High Command at War: Hindenburg and Ludendorff and the First World War*, William Morrow, London, 1991

Bond, B., & Cave, N. (eds), *Haig: A Reappraisal 70 Years On*, Leo Cooper/Pen and Sword, Barnsley, 1999

DeGroot, G., *Blighty: British Society in the era of the Great War*, Longman, London,1996.

Edmonds, Brig-Gen Sir J.E. (& Miles, Captain W.), *Military Operations: France and Belgium, 1914 (Volumes I and II), 1915 (Volumes I and II) and 1916 (Volumes I and II)*, MacMillan, London, 1922–38

Feldman, G., *Army, Industry and Labour in Germany, 1914–1918*, Princeton University Press, New Jersey, 1966

French, D., *British Strategy and War Aims, 1914–1916*, Allen and Unwin, London, 1986

Griffith, P., *Battle Tactics of the Western Front: The British Army's Art of Attack, 1916–18*, Yale University Press, London, 1994

Gundmundsson, B. *Stormtroop Tactics: Innovation in the German Army, 1914–1918*, Prager, New York, 1989

Holmes, R., *The Little Field Marshal: Sir John French* , Cape, London, 1981

Horne, A., *The Price of Glory: Verdun 1916*, Cape, London, 1962

Middlebrook, M., *The First Day on the Somme: 1 July 1916*, Allen Lane, London, 1971

Philpott, W., *Anglo-French Relations and Strategy on the Western Front, 1914–18*, MacMillan, London, 1996

Prior, R., & Wilson, T., *Command on the Western Front: The Military Career of Sir Henry Rawlinson 1914–18*, Blackwell, Oxford, 1992

Sheffield, G., *Forgotten Victory: The First World War, Myths and Realities*, Headline, London, 2001

Simkins, P., *Kitchener's Army: The Raising of the New Armies 1914–16*, Manchester University Press, 1988

Smith, L., *Between Mutiny and Obedience: The Case of the French Fifth Infantry Division during World War I* , Princeton University Press, New Jersey, 1994

Strachan, H., *The First World War: Volume I, To Arms*, Oxford University Press, 2001

Terraine, J., *Douglas Haig: The Educated Soldier*, Hutchinson, London, 1963

Williams, J., *The Home Fronts: Britain, France and Germany, 1914–1918* , Constable, London, 1972

Index

Other titles in the Essential Histories series

The Crusades
ISBN 1 84176 179 6

The Crimean War
ISBN 1 84176 186 9

**The Seven Years'
War**
ISBN 1 84176 191 5

**The Napoleonic
Wars** The rise of the
Emperor 1805–1807
ISBN 1 84176 205 9

**The Napoleonic
Wars** The empires fight
back 1808–1812
ISBN 1 84176 298 9

**The French
Revolutionary Wars**
ISBN 1 84176 283 0

**Campaigns of the
Norman Conquest**
ISBN 1 84176 228 8

**The American Civil
War** The war in the
East 1861–May 1863
ISBN 1 84176 239 3

**The American Civil
War** The war in the
West 1861–July 1863
ISBN 1 84176 240 7

**The American Civil
War** The war in the
East 1863–1865
ISBN 1 84176 241 5

**The American Civil
War** The war in the
West 1863–1865
ISBN 1 84176 242 3

The Korean War
ISBN 1 84176 282 2

The First World War
The Eastern Front
1914–1918
ISBN 1 84176 342 X
January 2002

The First World War
The Western Front
1914–1916
ISBN 1 84176 347 0
January 2002

**The Punic Wars
264–146 BC**
ISBN 1 84176 355 1
February 2002

**The Falklands
War 1982**
ISBN 1 84176 422 1
February 2002

**The Napoleonic
Wars** The Peninsular
War 1807–1814
ISBN 1 84176 370 5
March 2002

**The Second World
War** The Pacific
ISBN 1 84176 229 6
March 2002

**The Iran-Iraq War
1980–1988**
ISBN 1 84176 371 3
April 2002

**The Hundred Years'
War**
ISBN 1 84176 269 5
June 2002

The First World War
The Western Front
1916–1918
ISBN 1 84176 348 9
June 2002

Rome at War
AD 229–696
ISBN 1 84176 359 4
June 2002

The First World War
The Mediterranean
Front 1914–1923
ISBN 1 84176 373 X
July 2002

**The Second World
War** The Eastern Front
1941–1945
ISBN 1 84176 391 8
July 2002

**The Mexican War
1846–1848**
ISBN 1 84176 472 8
July 2002

Praise for Essential Histories

'clear and concise' *History Today*

'an excellent series' *Military Illustrated*

'Osprey must be congratulated on Essential Histories' *Soldier*

'very useful, factual and educational' *Reference Reviews*

'valuable as an introduction for students or younger readers ...
older readers will also find something 'essential' to their understanding' *Star Banner*

'accessible and well illustrated...' *Daily Express*

'... clearly written ...' *Oxford Times*

'they make the perfect starting point for readers of any age' *Daily Mail*

**The Wars of
Alexander the Great**
ISBN 1 84176 473 6
July 2002